D0689427

THE MYSTICAL ARTS OF TIBET

Featuring
PERSONAL SACRED OBJECTS OF H.H.
THE DALAI LAMA

❊

Text by Glenn H. Mullin and Andy Weber
Edited by Geshe Lobsang Tenzin Negi and Prof. Lloyd Nick
Exhibit Photographs by Bard Wrisley

Sponsored by Losel Shedrup Ling, Atlanta,
and the Richard Gere Foundation, New York

Co-sponsored by
OGLETHORPE UNIVERSITY MUSEUM
ATLANTA

LONGSTREET PRESS
Atlanta

Published by LONGSTREET PRESS, INC.,
a subsidiary of Cox Newspapers,
a subsidiary of Cox Enterprises, Inc.
2140 Newmarket Parkway
Suite 118
Marietta, Georgia 30067

Copyright © 1996 by Drepung Loseling Monastery and
Oglethorpe University Museum

All rights reserved. No part of this book may be reproduced in
any form by any means without the prior written permission of
the Publisher, excepting brief quotations used in connection
with reviews, written specifically for inclusion in a magazine or
newspaper.

Printed in the United States of America

1st printing, 1996

Library of Congress Catalog Number: 96-77398

ISBN Hardcover: 1-56352-352-3
ISBN Paperback: 1-56352-353-1

Digital film output and imaging by Overflow Graphics, Inc.
This book was printed by Quebecor / Hawkins Co. TN

Cover design by Jill Dible
Book design by Neil Hollingsworth
Cover photograph Dr. Lloyd Nick

Cover Image

Four-armed Avalokiteshvara

Size: 17″
Date: late 1500s

The four-armed form of Avalokiteshvara is the most popular with Tibetans of the 108 manifestations of the Bodhisattva of Compassion. The Dalai Lamas are incarnations of this form of him, and a search for a Dalai Lama reincarnation involves looking at the shoulders of the child for signs indicating the etheric presence of the second set of arms. The four arms represent the four immeasurable attitudes—love, compassion, experiencing only joy from the happiness of others, and equal concern for all living beings. His two inner hands hold a wish-fulfilling gem at his heart; the jewel represents compassion which brings only benefit to oneself and others. His left hand holds a mantra rosary, and with each bead that passes through his fingers a sentient being is freed from suffering. His right hand holds a lotus, symbolic of how compassion operates in the dark, muddy, ordinary world without becoming stained by worldly faults, just as a lotus grows in mud yet remains beautiful.

The face of the statue has been recently painted with gold. The bluish tint applied to the hair indicates that this was done within the last twenty years. It is a common practice to renew the gold paint on the face of an image every generation or so, as an act of offering and merit.

Tibetans of every school of Buddhism practice the mantra of Avalokiteshvara: *om mani padme hum*. *Om* represents the natural purity of body, speech, and mind; *mani* means jewel, and signifies compassion; *padme* means lotus, and signifies wisdom; and *hum* is a seal that establishes the power of compassion and wisdom in the mind of the mantra practitioner.

Part ONE :

PROFILE OF THE MYSTICAL ARTS OF TIBET

Part Two :

CATALOGUE OF THE EXHIBITION

Foreword by H.H. the Dalai Lama

Every culture has its distinguishing characteristics. For Tibetans, the emphasis has for many centuries been on developing and upholding inner values such as compassion and wisdom. These are more important for us than acquiring material wealth, fame, or success. We regard qualities such as inner strength, gentleness, love, compassion, wisdom, and a stable mind as the most important treasures a human being can collect in his or her lifetime. This is true wealth, benefiting ourselves and others, in the short term and long term. We have a saying in Tibetan that summarizes this wonderfully: "Inner jewels bring benefit in this life and the next." Ordinary wealth can bring as much harm as help, depending on how it is used. It is also easily lost. But inner jewels are always beneficial and cannot be lost. These inner jewels are the qualities symbolized in our paintings, statues, ritual implements, and so forth.

All the elements of a Tibetan religious painting have a symbolic value. These symbols serve as aids to developing inner qualities on the spiritual path. The deities themselves are regarded as representing particular characteristics of enlightenment. For example, Manjushri embodies wisdom and Avalokiteshvara embodies compassion. Paying respect to such deities therefore has the effect of paying respect to wisdom and compassion, which in turn functions as an inspiration to acquire those qualities ourselves.

The Chinese Communist invasion of Tibet has resulted in tremendous suffering and the deaths of more than a million Tibetans. The invaders have also indulged in cultural genocide. The decade-long Cultural Revolution saw the destruction of over 90 percent of our cultural artifacts. These included not only statues, paintings, and books, but even the buildings that housed them.

Following the Buddha's advice to help others if you can, or at the very least to avoid harming them, I have encouraged my people to pursue the path of nonviolence. We have not sought revenge for the destruction that has taken place. Fortunately, enough of our traditions have survived for us to set about a process of renewal. Those of us in exile have reestablished our monasteries and nunneries, we have reprinted our books, our artists have recreated works of art, and we have set about educating and training our young people. All these activities are a token of the Tibetan people's unbroken spirit to maintain their identity and culture.

Tibetan Buddhism has a distinctive contribution to make to the world's precious common heritage. I feel sure that the Drepung Loseling Monastery's *Mystical Arts of Tibet Sacred Music and Dance* tours and the accompanying exhibition of sacred art will deepen appreciation of our culture, both those themes that it has in common with other traditions and those aspects that make it unique.

I believe it is extremely important that we extend our understanding of each other's sacred traditions. This is not necessarily in order that we can adopt them ourselves, but because to do so increases our opportunities for mutual respect. Sometimes, too, we encounter something in another tradition that helps us better appreciate something in our own. After all, the fundamental aim of all religions is to help us to become better human beings and to create a happier, more peaceful world. It is my hope, therefore, that everyone visiting this exhibition may find in it inspiration and understanding that in some way contribute to their own inner peace.

June 8, 1996

Preface One

It gives me great pleasure, as director of Losel Shedrup Ling, the North American seat of Drepung Loseling Monastery in India, and also as director of The Mystical Arts of Tibet Foundation, finally to be able to put together this most wonderful exhibition of Tibetan art, centered around a collection of sacred objects belonging to His Holiness the Dalai Lama.

In 1987 two of the elders of Drepung Loseling Monastery, the late Khensur Yeshi Tupten and the then-abbot Rizong Rinpochey, felt that the efforts of the monastery to reestablish itself in India after its catastrophic destruction in Tibet by the Chinese Communists had achieved a satisfactory maturity and that the Loseling community could now consider looking beyond its immediate needs of self-preservation and begin to make efforts to contribute more visibly on an international basis. Their suggestion was that the monastery dispatch a world tour of lamas trained in the temple music and dances of Tibet, as a means of contributing to world peace and healing. In addition, their vision was that such an undertaking would increase world awareness of the situation in Tibet and raise funds for the preservation of Tibetan culture in exile. They approached Ven. Doboom Rinpochey, director of Tibet House in New Delhi, for advice on how to proceed. Rinpochey in turn asked his long-time friend and student Glenn H. Mullin, director of The Mystical Arts of Tibet Foundation and the author of numerous books on Tibetan culture, to take responsibility for the undertaking.

With the blessings of His Holiness the Dalai Lama, a group of lamas left India in September of 1988. Billed as "The Mystical Arts of Tibet: Sacred Music Sacred Dance for World Peace and Healing," over the following year it visited 108 cities in North America and 21 in Europe. It received an overwhelmingly warm response. The performances of ancient Tibetan Buddhist healing music and dances in theaters, festivals, universities, and churches met with full halls everywhere. The lamas met with Christian and Jewish church leaders, human rights activists, North American native elders, educators, artists and musicians, political leaders, and humanists; and they were received by governors, senators, congressmen, and mayors throughout their travels, many of whom issued official proclamations in appreciation of their efforts for world peace and in support of the Tibet issue. Then-governor Bill Clinton granted them Arkansas Goodwill Ambassadorships; Canadian Prime Minister Brian Mulrooney received them in a private audience; and they were given the keys to well over a dozen cities. The lamas spoke in several dozen universities and museums and appeared in hundreds of newspaper, radio, and television interviews. One of the CDs of their music, *Sacred Tibetan Temple Music*, even held a top twenty-five listing on the New Age music charts for over a year (2,500-year-old New Age music!).

The success of that early tour encouraged the monastery to continue to send lama groups abroad, and since that time four more one-year tours have taken place. Each of these has met with increasing success, and their schedule has been expanded to include South and Central America. Beginning with their second tour, in addition to presenting the traditional sacred performing arts, they began making sacred mandala sand paintings in museums and other venues as part of their activities, thus offering the international community a glimpse of this most extraordinary art.

The early tours were organized by Glenn H. Mullin in cooperation with a number of coordinators, most notably Ms. Lulu Hamlin of New York, Ms. Hilary Shearman of Toronto, Dr. Sandy Newhouse of Charlottesville, and Mr. Puntsok Wangyal of London. I had the honor and pleasure of serving as the spokesperson for the monastery on that first tour of 1988-89, and of co-directing the tours that followed.

In 1990 I accompanied His Eminence Rizong Rinpochey, abbot of Drepung Loseling, to the U.S.A. to accept officially a piece of land in north Georgia being offered to Loseling by Jim Kroeplin and Barbara Tucker. Rinpochey asked me to remain in America to oversee the development of a facility for Tibetan Buddhist studies and practice. I agreed on the basis that I could simultaneously pursue my personal studies in a local university. Ms. Lida Sims offered to provide accommodation to me for this purpose and to arrange for me to enter a Ph.D. program at Emory University. A scholarship enabling the fulfillment of this latter condition emerged thanks to the kindness of Prof. Robert Paul at Emory. This has worked out quite well for Drepung Loseling's outreach program; the small Tibetan Buddhist study center that formed in Atlanta in 1991 is now about to receive official affiliation with Emory University. This is very exciting for me, and means that we will soon be able to offer fully accredited courses in Tibetan Buddhist study through Emory.

In 1994 I was asked to accept the role of director of The Mystical Arts of Tibet Foundation, together with its ongoing projects of organizing tours by the monks of Drepung Loseling. Although I was hesitant to accept such a demanding and time-consuming commitment, I felt it important that the waves of auspicious activities that had previously been initiated and established be maintained, at least for as long as Tibetan culture continues to be oppressed in its homeland and its existence remains dependent upon a fragile refugee situation.

From the beginning of my work with the Foundation on our first world tour of 1988 I had wanted to bring over an exhibit of the sacred Tibetan fine arts. Although I very much appreciate the sacred performing arts and what was being done in this direction, I felt that there is a limit to the impact a group of lamas visiting a hundred cities in a year can have on any one particular venue and that it would be very beneficial to supplement these activities by organizing something that would more comprehensively reflect the cultural heritage of Tibet. With this in mind I discussed the possibilities of such an exhibit with the elders of the monastery. Together we approached His Holiness the Dalai Lama for his blessings, and asked if he felt it would be appropriate for us to create an exhibit featuring some of his personal sacred objects. His Holiness, a great advocate of world peace and a man who sincerely believes that Tibetan spiritual culture can make a significant contribution in this regard, graciously offered to provide us with a number of objects that are especially sacred to him and suitable to such an undertaking.

It has not been easy to arrange a sizable exhibit of this nature. The Chinese Communist invasion of Tibet and the destruction of so much of Tibet's ancient cultural heritage means that pieces of true antiquity and quality are extremely rare in the Tibetan community in exile. The Tibetan refugees escaping across the mountains into India often had to leave everything behind and come empty-handed. Fortunately, over the succeeding years a small number of H.H. the Dalai Lama's sacred belongings arrived in India with fleeing refugees, and were returned to him. In addition, a fraction of Drepung Loseling's collection was brought out in the early 1970s and was returned to the reestablished monastery in Mundgod. It is most wonderful that these can now be shared with a larger viewing public, and is an indication of the generosity and open-mindedness of His Holiness and the Tibetan elders in exile.

We have arranged the exhibit in three sections. The first of these is constituted of a selection of objects sacred to His Holiness the Dalai Lama. The second is drawn from the surviving collection of Drepung Loseling, the monastery to which the early Dalai Lamas belonged. The third section is comprised of a selection of contemporary pieces created by the refugees in India and Nepal, which serves to reflect the ongoing efforts of the Tibetans to preserve their ancient cultural heritage.

My success in bringing this project to fruition so quickly became possible mainly because of the kindness of His Holiness the Dalai Lama, the staff at his Private Office in Dharamsala, India, and the abbot and administrators at Drepung Loseling Monastery. In addition, I am deeply grateful to Mr. Rinchen Darlo of the Office of Tibet, New York, who is H.H. the Dalai Lama's representative in America, for his support, guidance, and valuable assistance.

Dr. Lloyd Nick, director of the Oglethorpe University Museum and head of the art department at Oglethorpe University, has been invaluable in helping to bring the exhibit together. I was delighted when he expressed an interest in having O.U.M. act as a co-sponsor of the exhibit. He threw himself enthusiastically into the project, brought his expertise into the work, and gave much wise advice that helped the undertaking to succeed. In addition he was instrumental in finding corporate sponsorships and arranged for the publication of our catalog. He succeeded also in arranging for the first showing of the exhibit to be held at Oglethorpe University Museum, Atlanta, in celebration of the Summer Olympics.

I am indebted to Richard Gere for co-sponsoring this exhibit with us and would like to thank both him and his staff at the Richard Gere Foundation in New York for their encouragement and support.

Bard Wrisley, one of Georgia's most talented and respected photographers, very kindly donated his valuable time and talents in order to prepare the images of the exhibit objects used in this book. The master artist and Tibetan art historian Andy Weber kindly took time from his busy schedule and flew from his home in England in order to provide us with his expertise in correctly identifying and dating the individual objects and helping Glenn write the text of our catalog. His assistance and knowledge have been invaluable.

The original concept for this exhibit belongs to Ms. Lida Sims, and from the earliest moments of its inception she has provided constant input that has helped shape the form that the project has taken. I would also like to thank the staff and sangha at Losel Shedrup Ling, Atlanta, for their many hours of volunteer work in helping to bring it all together; and also Ms. Debby Spencer, who worked as our artistic consultant.

I am especially indebted to Ms. Jane Moore and Mr. Michael Hellbach of the Tibet Image Bank, London, for providing us with the photographs that appear in Part One of this book. These photos are part of a selection from the Tibet Image Bank that will travel with our exhibition in order to illustrate the social context within which Tibetan art developed and thrived. The photographers of the individual images are listed at the end of the book.

Finally, I would like to thank Glenn H. Mullin, not only for writing the text of this publication, but also for helping with ideas and concepts throughout the formation of the project. In fact, he has in many ways been the real coordinator of this exhibit.

In conclusion, the actual inspiration for my organizing this exhibit derives from His Holiness the Dalai Lama and his request that everyone make whatever effort he or she can strengthen the forces of peace, nonviolence, and goodness in the world. It is my sincere wish that this exhibit will make a contribution in this direction and that all who see it will be moved by the Tibetan culture of love, compassion, and wisdom.

Geshe Lobsang Tenzin Negi
Director
The Mystical Arts of Tibet

Preface Two: The Art of Enlightenment

In ordinary life creativity means making something for the soul out of every experience. As the poets and painters of centuries have tried to tell us, art is not about the expression of talent or the making of pretty things: It is about the preservation and containment of the soul. It is about arresting and making it available for contemplation. Art captures the eternal in the everyday, and it is the eternal that feeds the soul the whole world in a grain of sand.

Thomas Moore, *Care of the Soul*

This exhibit of the mystical art of Tibet is not only highly educational, it is truly magical.

Art is an effort to formalize individual moments of wholeness, harmony, and radiance. The transcending effects of these moments, the energy which discloses the mystery of the universe in responding to our spiritual curiosity, uplift and satisfy the soul's need to question and to speak. The tenderness and the powerful presence of art create an inner sunlit circle in which one is quiet and elated. It is a moment of magic.

This exhibit of the mystical art of Tibet is such a crystallized moment. In art and in spiritual life neutrality does not exist. The greatest artists have been magicians, alchemists transforming ordinary pigments, stone, and metal through their sustaining passion. Layered colored oils by Rembrandt or chiseled marble blocks by Michelangelo, a sonnet by Shakespeare, or a haiku poem by Basho, they make the pure experience of beauty transparent. When we see such pieces of art, they ring like a bell in us forever. We never forget this delicate, gentle sensation of enlightenment. It raises us to a new level of being which we can never relinquish.

This collection contains not just one or two pieces that will bring the viewer to that heightened emotional level; almost every piece contains the ability to ring that special bell of our personal growth.

Where would a patron of the arts be able to find a twelfth-century ceremonial dagger that has been used steadily only by holy men who have instilled in it extraordinary powers that are felt by those who see it today; or the Dalai Lama's saffron robe and cherry-colored carnelian mala (prayer beads), witnesses of ritual and earnest meditation; or the thanka painting of the Dalai Lama's guardian angel sent by the gods to secure the reincarnation of the Dalai Lama and serving as a protector of all Tibetans?

Sacred objects and images are artistically rendered vehicles that connect our human world with the realm of Spirit and make the radiant self within more palpable. It is my feeling that the profound echoes of this exhibit will compare to the aesthetic influence of the first contact of Western art with the art and sensibility of Japan in the second half of the last century. This time, however, the paradigm is at a spiritual level.

I believe that many who see this exhibit, as it travels for the next five years, will be changed. This is a wealth of information about an area of life the West has all but blocked out yet we all have yearned to know. This group of sacred objects will mesmerize the viewer into a deeper personal level of universal awareness.

Oglethorpe University Museum is honored to be co-sponsor of this exhibit. It is a responsibility we accept with humility and gratitude. Through the kind support of Swissair and its General Manager for Southeast USA, Eberhard Suhr, the exhibit items reached their destination; Longstreet Press and its publisher and editor, Chuck Perry, solidified our vision of an important event by publishing this catalog. It has been a pleasure to work with

Geshe Lobsang Tenzin Negi, who organized the exhibition; Glenn Mullin, the catalog's author; Andy Weber, the catalog's artistic adviser; and the photographer, Bard Wrisley, who captured tastefully the images for the catalog. I am grateful to my associate at O.U.M. Kathleen Guy,who also shared in and has worked toward this vision, and to the students and the many volunteers in the Atlanta community who contributed selflessly.

Working on such creative projects changes lives.

Lloyd Nick
Director, Oglethorpe University Museum

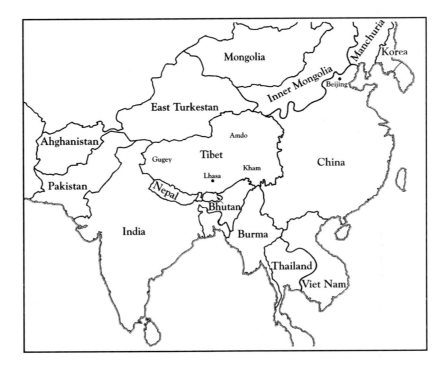

A Technical Note

Written Tibetan is laden with silent prefix, suffix, superscript, and subscript letters that function only to change the pronunciation of the related vowels and consonants with which they appear. For example, mKhas-grub-rje is actually pronounced as Khedrub Jey, and gNas-brtan-bcu-drug as Neyten Chudruk. Because this publication is designed for the general public, we have rendered all Tibetan names and terms in accordance with how they sound, and not how they are more formally transliterated. mKhas-grub-rje and gNas-brtan-bcu-drug are undecipherable and meaningless to the general reader. Specialist will know the more formal spellings, or at least be able to look them up if they are sufficiently interested.

Similarly, Sanskrit names and terms are Anglicized; an academic treatment involving diacritic marks would just distract the general reader; again, the specialist will know the more formal renderings without our assistance.

We have not belabored the text with footnotes. Instead, a bibliography is provided for those interested in pursuing the subjects discussed.

PART ONE

PROFILE OF THE MYSTICAL ARTS OF TIBET

CHAPTER ONE

REFLECTIONS ON THE TIBET STORY

Photo credit © TIB

Lhasa

BETWEEN THE BRUSH STROKES

The art of a people tells a great deal about their character, worldview, attitudes, hopes, and aspirations. Their history is reflected in it, as is their basic psychological orientation, direction, and aesthetic sensitivity.

Tibetan art for the past thirteen hundred years has been dedicated to the expression of the Buddhist mystical passion. It tells a story that at once is both meditative in focus and profoundly spiritual in texture. It is not "creative" in the modern Western sense, but rather is expressive of the discipline and mythology of the enlightenment experience. It celebrates the great beings of the past who have achieved enlightenment, the fundamental means by which that experience is induced, and the traditional symbolism that has been developed and refined over centuries of continuous efforts by its lineage masters, artists, writers, and philosophers. It brings ancient legends into the present and breathes a new life and meaning into them, carrying the voices of the ancestors into the here-and-now in such a way as to facilitate a continuity and evolution of a social and cultural identity.

To truly appreciate the artistic forms of a culture, we have to cultivate a working knowledge of their secret language. Only then do they reveal their inner hidden beauties to us and become part of what we are.

The language of Tibetan art is a combination of a number of important elements that fused over the millenniums. In the end the Buddhism of India became the predominant force; but traces of the ancient culture continued, as did influences from Persia, Mongolia, China, and other of Tibet's neighbors.

This book is not just a catalog of an exhibit, but rather is an introduction to the artistic history of Tibet and the world of its mysticism. It attempts to look into the heart and spirit of the unique

Nomad with prayer wheel

and ancient culture of Tibet as reflected in its artwork. The wisdom, compassion, and profound humanity demonstrated by the Dalai Lama—qualities for which he has become such an internationally loved and respected figure—are flowers that blossomed from the fertile soil of a civilization that stretches back in time over many centuries. What follows is a sketch of that civilization.

The Geographical Setting

Tibet is often referred to in popular Western literature as "The Roof of the World," for even its fertile valleys, where most of its six million inhabitants live, lie at an altitude of more than 12,000 feet above sea level. Many of its mountain ranges tower to altitudes of well over 20,000 feet. The Himalayas, with Mt. Everest as its crown jewel, stretch over the southern border like a natural fence of snow and ice; the Kun Lun and Tangla ranges stand to the north; the Karakoram and Ladakh mountains, including the holy Mt. Kailash, block off the west; and the hills and high grasslands of Kham and Amdo protect the east.

Traditional Asian songs refer to Tibet as the Land of Snow Mountains and the source of glacial waters. Indeed, many of Asia's great rivers do flow from Tibet's glacial mountains. To name but a few, the Indus of Pakistan, the Ganges and Brahmaputra of India, and the Yangtse and Mekong of China, all are born within the Land of Snow Mountains. When one flies into Lhasa from any direction one sees its great rivers winding like diamond ribbons from valley to valley, steadily making their way out of the mountains and onto the plains of the neighboring lowlands.

However, only twenty-five million years ago the area that is now Tibet lay at the bottom of the sea. Then the continental shelfs of the world began to shift. They collided together, causing a great buckling at their point of impact. Even today sea coral and shellfish fossils are to be found in Tibet's remote caves and valleys, frozen in time since that ancient era.

Sometimes we see it said that Tibet was a small Himalayan kingdom; in fact, it was over a million square miles in size, which is larger than the entirety of Western Europe. However, it is important to realize that Tibet as a cultural region was far larger than these political borders. For many centuries now it has served as the spiritual, cultural, and artistic fountainhead for much of Central Asia. Modern anthropologists speak of a "Tibetan ethnographic area," which extends from Siberia, Buriatia, and Mongolia in the north to the Himalayan kingdoms of Nepal, Sikkim, Bhutan, and Himalayan India in the south; and from Ladakh, Lahoul, Spitti, and Kinnaur in the west to the Tartar regions of Manchuria and China in the east. This "ethnographic Tibet" covers an area almost as large as the United States of America.

The Dalai Lamas of Tibet have for some five centuries been regarded as the most important spiritual leaders in this vast region.

Tibet's Lopa Aboriginals

The roots of Tibetan civilization are to be found in the border regions of Tibet and Burma. Linguistically, the Tibetan language is said to belong to the Tibeto-Burmese family. The peoples of this region slowly increased in population,

with many of them migrating northward, until eventually they came to populate the valleys of Central Asia, the most important of these being Zhangzhung and Yarlung. As the centuries passed they traded, fought, and interbred with various of their neighbors, bringing many differ-

Photo credit © TIB

Tibetan maiden

ent genetic, linguistic, and cultural traits into their civilization; but the basic foundation remained Tibeto-Burmese.

Many anthropologists believe that the indigenous peoples of the Americas are descended from a nomadic tribe of these same tribesmen, who migrated across the Bering Strait some 15,000 to 20,000 years ago. Modern genetic studies seem to reinforce this belief.

A little known fact among Western Tibetologists is that several tribes of Tibetans having many cultural characteristics similar to those of our North American natives survived almost unchanged into the present century, at least up until the Chinese invasion. Tibetans refer to these tribes as Lopa. The Lopa wore feather headdresses, hunted with bows and arrows, and painted their faces with fierce designs in times of battle.

In 1986 a group of lamas from Gyumey Tantric College were in North America to perform their sacred music in university theaters. While in Ottawa, Canada, they were invited to visit the Museum of Man, which had an exhibit of native artworks on display. After a half hour in the museum, the head lama suggested that we leave. When asked if he found the material uninteresting, he replied, "We didn't come halfway around the world to see our own things." He had grown up near a tribe of Lopa and thought that the Native American artwork in the museum was from his homeland in Tibet.

A group of lamas from Drepung Loseling Monastery on a tour of sacred music and dance was in Santa Fe, New Mexico, in 1988. The photographer Marcia Keegan had arranged a showing of her work in the Governor's Gallery in honor of their visit to town. She had set two images in each frame: one depicting an aspect of New Mexican Pueblo native culture; and one an aspect of Tibetan culture. The governor and our head lama walked hand-in-hand through the gallery, testing one another by trying to guess which image represented which culture. The similarities were so strong that both guessed wrong as many times as right.

Of course, Marcia had focused her exhibit on features of the two peoples that show strong cultural similarities. These are most clearly evident in the culture of Tibet's Lopa tribes; but elements of them continue in substratum throughout the later periods.

During this same visit to Santa Fe the lamas were invited to witness an annual sacred dance being done by one of the Pueblo nations. The symbolism of the dance was explained to our head lama during the ceremony. He too had known several Tibetan tribes of Lopa, and commented that they also had an annual dance ceremony that was almost identical in both form and symbolism to that of the Pueblo.

Unfortunately, no study of the Lopa was done prior to the 1950s, and it may now be too late.

THE BON PERIOD

Long before the West witnessed the birth of Christ, Tibet was swept by a religious movement that came in from a land they call Tazig, which probably refers to ancient Persia. The movement took root in the Zhangzhung Valley, located in western Tibet near Mt. Kailash, and then spread eastward. Tibetans refer to it as the Bon religion.

The nature of original Bon is probably lost to history, for the Tibetans of this early period had no written script of their own or, even if they did, no text from the period has survived. The oldest Bon scripture extant today dates from the late ninth century A.D., long after Buddhism had already taken a firm foothold in the Land of Snows. Moreover, with the arrival of Buddhism in the seventh century, Bon became so utterly transformed by the Buddhist experience that it became almost unrecognizable as a separate entity. It has survived, of course, and there are Bonpo monasteries today in both India and Nepal; but how close the philosophy and practice of contemporary Bon is to the Bon of the pre-Buddhist period is a matter of conjecture.

The dating of events in this early period is extremely tentative. Bon history is written in a mythological language and has no difficulty in speaking in terms of tens of thousands of years. Their texts describe their founder as Tonpa Sherab, and some speak of him as being an early incarnation of the soul that later was to become the Buddha.

Prof. David Snellgrove points out in *The Nine Ways of Bon* that the form of Bon that encountered Buddhism in the mid-seventh century was very possibly already strongly influenced by the Buddhism of Kashmir, and may even simply have been an early form of Kashmiri tantric Buddhism. This would date the Bon founder Tonpa Sherab much later than most Bonpo scholars would like; but there may be some validity to the theory.

Both the Lopa and Bon are usually described in Western literature as being "animistic," a term that has both a condescending and somewhat derogatory tone to it, and at the same time con-

veys very little real meaning. The word is used by Buddhologists to distinguish the Lopa and Bon traditions from Buddhism in Tibet. However, given the standard definition of animism as a belief system that sees all phenomena as pulsating with life, tantric Buddhism could easily be said to be equally animistic. It too sees the earth, moon, sun, and stars as being the bodies of deities; and it holds that trees, rivers, winds, and fire can become host to a plethora of nature spirits and etheric forms.

Tantric Buddhism is rich in "animist" rituals. For example, when the Dalai Lama gave the Kalachakra initiation in Ladakh in 1976, he sent his ritual rainmaker/rainstopper three weeks in advance, with the instruction to create a good cloud cover over the Ladakhi skies during the time of the initiation. The tantric belief is that wind spirits control rainfall and clouds, and also the lack of them. Ladakh rarely has clouds at that time of year, and His Holiness feared that the tens of thousands of people who would attend, and who would have to sit in the open for the week-long teachings and initiation, would become scorched in the high-altitude sun. However, the clouds also brought some rain, and the crowd complained strongly to the rainmaker lama. The rainmaker replied that he could give them sun and dry weather, or he could give them clouds with the occasional rain; but at that altitude he could not give them clouds with no rain. The crowd opted for the sun, and the weather lama immediately changed his rituals. Within a few hours the clouds were gone and everyone was burning in the sun.

Some Western scholars, with little knowledge

of Indian tantric traditions and less of Tibetan history, have suggested that these forms of Tibetan Buddhist practice are "corruptions" that crept into Tibetan Buddhism from Tibet's early "animist" traditions. Even a cursory glance at Indian Buddhist tantric literature reveals that this is not the case. If anything, Tibetan practices of this nature point to a more ancient shamanic root shared by a number of pan-Asian spiritual legacies. One can find rituals of this nature in the ancient Lopa and Bon traditions of Tibet, in the shamanism of Siberia and Mongolia, in the Taoism of China, and in the tantric traditions of India.

Prayer flags in a mountain pass

Photo credit © TIB

THE BODHISATTVA OF COMPASSION, AN ABOMINABLE SNOWLADY, AND TIBET'S FIRST KING

Kachen Yeshey Gyaltsen, one of the greatest masters of the mid-eighteenth century and the guru of the Eighth Dalai Lama, makes an interesting observation in his account of the legends of Avalokiteshvara, the Buddha of Compassion. The passage captures a number of ancient Tibetan beliefs that had been recorded in a text by the early Kadampa lamas seven centuries earlier, known as *Pacho Bucho*, or *Father Dharmas Son Dharmas*.

The first of these distinctly Tibetan beliefs is that the Buddha of Compassion has since time immemorial played a special role in Tibetan affairs; that the Tibetan race is descended from a cross between a monkey and an abominable snowlady, with the monkey in fact being an emanation of the Bodhisattva of Compassion; and that Tibet's first king was an emanation of that same buddha form.

Kachen Yeshey Gyaltsen writes this very story:

The bodhisattva Avalokiteshvara looked down on Tibet from his abode in the Potala Pure Land. In the upper western regions of Ngari, he beheld beautiful mountain regions filled with deer, antelope, and mountain goats. Below, in Tsang, he beheld rocky hills and pastures filled with deer and monkeys. In the east, in Kham and Amdo, he beheld grassy plains and thick forests filled with various types of primates.

He saw many auspicious signs in the Land of Snow Mountains, and therefore took birth there as a monkey. Simultaneously, his divine female emanation Tara took birth as an abominable snowlady. The two of them joined together, and their union produced the first six human beings. These children were each of a different color and complexion. They rapidly increased in number, until the entire land was populated. . . .

Many ages went by, and again Avalokiteshvara looked down. He saw that his decsendants had turned from the ways of peace and had transformed the land of beauty into a realm pervaded by the sufferings like those of a hell realm. Therefore, over a period of many generations, he emanated a thousand incarnations, and these took birth among the people and taught them the ways of harmony. In this way he brought the enlightenment tradition to the Land of Snows, and made it into a celestial garden.

One of these emanations took birth in India as the princely son of King Maggyapa. This child possessed all the signs of being blessed by the saints, such as having webbed hands, turquoise eyes, teeth like conch shells, and the impressions of wheels on his hands. However, his father mistook these omens as indicating that the baby was a demon incarnate, and therefore placed him in a casket and threw him in the river. Yet fate would not allow the child to die before his task had been accomplished. Light rays from the wisdom beings protected him, and eventually guided him to his destiny in Tibet. He arrived at Yarlha Shampo Mountain, descending from the sky by means of a rope ladder.

It is here that the Tibetans first encountered him and made him their king. . . .

The story of the monkey and abominable snowlady giving birth to the first humans in Tibet probably has its origins in aboriginal Lopa legend that later was amended to a Buddhist context.

The Buddhist tradition of the bodhisattva Avalokiteshvara achieved great popularity in the Land of Snows from its earliest Buddhist days, and eventually Tibetan history was reinterpreted, with Avalokiteshvara becoming associated with every major event. Thus we see him here portrayed as the genetic forefather of the six early Tibetan races.

Tibetans date their birth as a nation to the fourth century B.C., when an exiled Indian prince whom they call Nyatri Tsenpo arrived in the Yarlung Valley. Again, the above quotation reveals how the Tibetans also regarded him as an emanation of the bodhisattva Avalokiteshvara.

Popular legend states that the local Tibetans first encountered Nyatri Tsenpo on Mt. Shampo. They were profoundly impressed by his appearance and demeanor and asked him from where he had come. Unable to understand their language, he just pointed his fingers upward and turned his wrist counterclockwise to indicate his noncomprehension, a hand gesture still widely used today in India to indicate confusion. They mistook the upward-pointing fingers to mean that he was claiming to be a god who had descended from the heavens. The name they gave him, Nyatri Tsenpo, means "Palanquin-born Lord," for they placed him on a palanquin, carried him back to their village, and made him their king.

One Tibetan account goes so far as to claim that Nyatri Tsenpo was descended from the Shakya clan, to which the Buddha himself had belonged. Another claims him as a descendant of the Pandava brothers, who are the heros of the great Indian classic *The Mahabharata*, of which the *Bhagavadgita* is a summary.

Some Western scholars have suggested that the legend of Nyatri Tsenpo could mean that he was an Indian prince who had been part of

The Bodhisattva of Compassion

Photo credit © TIB

a defeated army in India's ongoing internal petty wars and had fled India over the Himalayas in order to escape capture. Eventually he and his small army arrived in the Yarlung Valley, where they settled and gradually brought the neighboring tribes under their control. Within a few generations of intermarriage with the local Tibetans, they had lost all traces of their Indian ancestry.

There is also the possibility that King Nyatri Tsenpo had no Indian blood whatsoever, and that this legend was built up around him many centuries later by Tibet's Buddhist historians in their enthusiasm for and glorification of everything Indian, in order to add to his aura. Later Tibetan religious historians list Nyatri Tsenpo as a previous incarnation of the soul that was to become the Dalai Lama.

Be this as it may, he and his descendants were enthusiastic builders, and the dynasty that he established lasted for almost a thousand years, until it eventually encompassed the entirety of Central Asia.

Nyatri Tsenpo constructed a castle in the Yarlung Valley that became the headquarters for himself and his ancestors, and that marked what was to serve as the capital of Tibet from his time until the mid-seventh century A.D., when King Songtsen Gampo,

Photo credit © TIB

The site of Tibet's first castle

empire and in importing Buddhism and establishing it as the national religion of the country. Again, Tibetan religious histories speak of all three of these kings as having been previous incarnations of the Dalai Lamas.

The tradition of identifying the Dalai Lamas as later reincarnations of these three Dharma kings is based on a book of prophecies by an Indian master known as Atisha Dipamkara Shrijnana, who came to Tibet in 1042 and taught there until his death a decade and a half later. His chief disciple was a layman known as Lama Drom Tonpa. Atisha made many prophecies about previous and future incarnations of Lama Drom. Included in the previous incarnations were thirty-six Indian lives, each of which Atisha recounted in detail. He also mentioned ten previous incarnations of Lama Drom as kings of Tibet, the most important of these being the Three Great Dharma Kings. Four centuries later the First Dalai Lama came to be recognized as a reincarnation of Lama Drom, and as a consequence all the "previous incarnations of Lama Drom" of which Atisha had spoken came to be regarded as previous incarnations of the Dalai Lamas.

the thirty-third king of the Yarlung Dynasty, constructed the Red Fortress in the Lhasa Valley and made Lhasa his new capital.

The successive kings of the Yarlung Dynasty soon embraced the Bon religion, which seems to have been pervasive throughout Tibet from the earliest days of their rule.

THE THREE GREAT DHARMA KINGS AND THE ADVENT OF BUDDHISM

The period of the mid-seventh to the mid-ninth centuries A.D. are known as the era of the Three Great Dharma Kings: Songtsen Gampo, Trisong Deutsen, and Tri Ralpachen. These three were instrumental in both consolidating the Tibetan

KING SONGTSEN GAMPO, HIS FIVE WIVES, AND TIBET'S FIRST BUDDHIST TEMPLES

Many of Atisha's prophecies are woven into his accounts of Lama Drom's previous lives in India. For example, in one of them, *The Incarnation as Prince Ratna Das*, he tells the story of Lama Drom as a young Indian prince called Ratna Das who travels to Oddiyana (modern-day Swat, Pakistan) in search of secret teachings. On the way he meets a mystical female, Guhyajnana by name, who speaks the following words:

> In future you will incarnate in Tibet as
>   many kings
> And introduce the ways of the enlighten-
>   ment tradition,
> Bringing civilization to that remote land.
> During one of your royal incarnations
> I will take birth as a princess in China
> And you will summon me to be your queen.
> Although in reality an incarnation of the
>   bodhisattva Tara
> And therefore beyond all worldly illusions,
> Nonetheless I will play the role of one of
>   your queens
> In order to bring benefits to others. . . .
> I will carry numerous objects of faith to
>   Tibet
> And place them in a site like an eight-
>   petaled lotus,
> The sky above like an eight-spoked wheel
>   of truth,
> Surrounded by mountains with the eight
>   auspicious signs.
> There, in your kingdom adorned with these
>   mystical signs,

> We will make good karma together
> And inspire songs of spiritual joy.
> I, Guhyajnana, mystical female of secret
>   wisdom,
> Sing this wisdom song to you now.
> Listen to it, O son of a king.

This prophecy refers to the first of the Three Great Dharma Kings, Songtsen Gampo, the thirty-third monarch in the Yarlung Dynasty descending from Nyatri Tsenpo, and the Chinese princess who became one of his wives.

King Songtsen Gampo is remembered in the annals of Tibetan history with particular enthusiasm, because not only did he vastly expand Tibet's borders, drawing within his empire large territories from Northern India, Nepal, Bhutan, Western China, Chinese Turkestan, Kashmir, and Pakistan, but also because he laid the foundations for the flowing of the enlightenment tradition of India into Tibet on a grand scale. Tibetan civilization as we know it today is very much based in Songtsen Gampo's work.

Songtsen Gampo married five princesses from various regions of Asia in order to foster peace within and around his borders. Two of these were non-Tibetans and were Buddhist. The first of these was Princess Bhikuti from Nepal, whom he married in 637 A.D., and the second was Princess Wencheng, from China, whom he married in 641. Tibetan histories explain that his two Buddhist queens so profoundly impressed him that not only did he convert to Buddhism himself, but passed decrees that in effect made Buddhism the national religion of the country.

Tibetans tell the story of Songtsen Gampo's relationship with the two princesses in various

Photo credit © TIB

The Jokhang, Tibet's first Buddhist temple

ways. One somewhat humorous account relates that the princesses were distraught with the harshness and vulgarity of their mountain barbarian husband and refused to sleep with him until he polished his ways. This embarrassed him considerably, and he decided that the only solution was for him to educate himself in the subtleties and refinements of the high civilizations of India and China, which meant learning Buddhism. He threw himself into the study and practice with vigor, and eventually managed to convince his Buddhist queens that he had become a gentleman. His marital life returned to normal, and they lived happily every after. The Lhasa area is dotted with caves and temples

where Songtsen and his two Buddhist queens practiced meditation together.

For each of the two queens, he constructed a grand temple in which they could continue the practice of their devotions and house the holy images that they had brought with them to Tibet. For the Nepali princess, he erected the Jokhang in 640, which today is regarded as Lhasa's oldest and holiest temple. Its door faces toward the southwest, the direction of the land of her birth. A few years later he constructed the Ramochey Temple for his Chinese queen, its door facing east, toward the land of her birth.

By an interesting twist of fate, after the Chinese Communist invasion of Tibet in the

1950s, the People's Liberation Army confused the origins of the two temples and the princesses for whom they had been built. Wishing to erase the memory of the Nepali queen, and to enhance the stature of the Chinese queen, the Chinese destroyed the Ramochey and declared the Jokhang to be Lhasa's main temple. Their design was to imply that Tibet had become part of China in 641 with the marriage of Emperor Songtsen Gampo to Princess Wenchen, and to eradicate any overt evidence of his earlier marriage to Princess Brikuti in 637, which presumably they saw as an inconvenience to their rewrite of history. As a result, the temple that had been built for the Chinese princess was destroyed.

In addition to these two large temples, Songtsen had 108 smaller temples built at various power places throughout the country in order to bind the spirits of the earth to the path of goodness and enlightenment. This was a most significant period in the development of Tibetan art, for all of these temples were equipped with numerous religious artifacts in order to make them into places of devotion and pilgrimage.

Another lasting work initiated by Emperor Songtsen Gampo was his effort in sending a group of Tibetans to India in order to devise a script and grammar suitable for the translation of Buddhist texts into Tibetan. Prior to his time Tibet had subsisted on borrowed scripts, with Persian being used in the western provinces, Chinese in the eastern, Kotanese in the northern, and so forth. To accomplish this, he sent Tomi Sambhota with sixteen assistants to India to research the situation. The phonetic script that they devised was based on a simplified form of Gupta Sanskrit and has endured until the present day. The three scriptures included in our exhibition, *The Mystical Arts of Tibet*, are penned in this same script.

Tibetans like to tell the story of Songtsen Gampo's dedication to Buddhism in a way that implies he was motivated purely by spiritual considerations. However, it is also possible that he felt that his newlyestablished empire could only endure as a political entity if it was also united linguistically, culturally, and spiritually. He must have been impressed by the sophisticated civilizations that thrived in the countries surrounding Tibet, all of which were Buddhist and large parts of which he now ruled; perhaps he saw in Buddhism a sophisticated and unifying tradition that would serve as the golden thread that would tie together his life's works.

KING TRISONG DEUTSEN, GURU PADMA SAMBHAVA, AND TIBET'S FIRST MONASTERY

A hundred years later the second great Dharma king appeared. This was King Trisong Deutsen, who brought the illustrious tantric master Guru Padma Sambhava from India, sponsored the building of Tibet's first monastery, Samyey, and greatly furthered the translation of Buddhist texts from Sanskrit into Tibetan.

He was also a very powerful ruler. Like his ancestor Songtsen Gampo, he took a large number of princesses as wives in order to ensure stable relationships with his internal and external allies. When he demanded a senior princess from the Chinese court and was refused, he invaded

China, captured the Chinese capital, and held it for several months until his wishes were met. He even temporarily displaced the Chinese emperor in 763 and installed another in his place. During Trisong Deutsen's reign China had to pay a tribute to Tibet of 50,000 rolls of silk annually.

His relationship with the Indian tantric master guru Padma Sambhava (see pages 76 and 77) has been immortalized in thousands of myths and legends. It is said that when the great guru first arrived in Lhasa the king hesitated in bowing to him, feeling it more appropriate that Padma Sambhava bow to him, the king. The great guru pointed at him and sent a blast of flame from his fingers that set the king's clothing on fire. The king immediately bowed and became his disciple.

Padma Sambhava was not a monk. Quite to the contrary, he was a tantric master who is said to have seduced every woman that he could in order to bring higher incarnations into the world. Like Prince Krishna of ancient India, who allegedly made love to 16,000 women during his lifetime, Padma Sambhava's romantic conquests numbered in the thousands. Knowing the guru's admiration for beautiful women, King Trisong Deutsen offered him his most beautiful Tibetan queen, Yeshey Tsogyal, as a consort dur-

Guru Padma Sambhava

Photo credit © TIB

ing his sojourn in Tibet. Again, she has become the subject of legend, and is said to be the first Tibetan woman to have achieved full enlightenment. Her meditations and travels with Guru Padma Sambhava, and her romantic relationship with him, fill volumes of Tibetan texts. Most of these are not histories or biographies in the conventional sense, but are "treasure texts," perceived by mystics centuries later in dreams or meditation, and accordingly transcribed.

King Trisong Deutsen's contribution to the arts was monumental, and during his reign he filled the valleys and mountains of Tibet with many of the greatest artisans from India, Nepal, Kotan, and China. They built temples and filled them with paintings, sculptures, metal works, and decorative symbols that greatly influenced the artists of all future generations. In brief, he took the artistic foundations laid by Songtsen Gampo and carried them to an unprecedented level of achievement.

The relationship between the great Guru and Queen Yeshey Tsogyal is immortalized in numerous texts, several of which have been translated into English. The stories of their exploits are filled with magic, mystery, fun, and laughter. They rarely walked anywhere, but instead simply transformed their bodies into rainbow energy and flew through the skies at the speed of thought. There is no real history of their lives and accomplishments in the Western academic sense; instead we have a vast collection of "treasure texts" created many centuries later by mystics and clairvoyants. This does not, to the Tibetans, render the accounts of their lives and deeds any less valid or real.

Before leaving Tibet, Padma Sambhava made an extensive tour throughout the country, consecrating and empowering the lakes, rivers, mountains, and caves by means of his presence and his tantric rituals. King Trisong Deutsen traveled with him on many of these excursions, receiving the secret, esoteric doctrines from him.

The king personally established twelve meditation centers around the country for the use of his people, the three most famous being those at Chimpu, Yerpa, and Pal Chuwori. He is said to have dedicated much of his time to the practice of meditation in order to set an example for his people.

A very significant event to take place during Trisong Deutsen's life affected the direction that Buddhism in Tibet was to take over the course of the succeeding centuries, namely, the great debate between the Indian and Chinese factions of Buddhist monks.

The exact cause of the conflict between the two is unclear. Most Tibetan accounts interpret it as having been based in the philosophical differences between the Chinese Ch'an and the Indian Mahayana/Vajrayana schools. The statement usually given is that the Ch'an monks were teaching a form of meditation known in Tibetan

Samyey, Tibet's first monastery

as *chila yang mila mi chepai gom*, which translates as "doing absolutely nothing in the mind." In other words, it was a form of suppression of thoughts. The situation was expressed by Hvashang Mahayana, the head Ch'an monk as follows: "Both white clouds and black clouds obstruct the sun. He who has no thoughts at all achieves liberation from cyclic existence." Also, the sociological implication was that good and evil actions were equally meaningless, for both were ultimately nonexistent and conventionally distorted. The Indian Buddhist position was that even though ultimately nothing really exists, on the conventional level there is a big difference between black and white clouds, and between good and evil. Moreover, the Indians regarded Hvashang Mahayana's meditative techniques as being the mere suppression of mental activity, and not the unleashing of wisdom.

In that these two schools had happily co-existed in various places in Central Asia for several centuries, including in Lhasa for over a hundred years, the thesis that the conflict was born from philosophical differences is unconvincing. More probably it had to do with a wish on the part of the Tibetan rulers to find an excuse to oust the Chinese monks from Tibet, whom they suspected of political intrigue.

In any case, the great debate took place in Lhasa in 792. The Chinese faction lost, all Chinese monks were expelled from the country, and Tibet declared itself officially a cultural satellite of Buddhist India. This was of considerable significance to the arts, for Tibet now began to look almost exclusively to the south and west for its artistic inspiration and direction.

KING TRI RALPACHEN, THE LAST GREAT DHARMA KING

The third of the Three Great Dharma Kings is Tri Ralpachen, who reigned from 817 to 836 A.D. He was Trisong Deutsen's grandson, and the last great Buddhist king of Lhasa in the early period.

His uncle Muney Tsenpo had succeeded King Trisong Deutsen to the throne and had the unusual distinction of attempting three times to establish a material equality with all his subjects. Three times all wealth and property were confiscated and divided equally between his subjects, but on each occasion these found their way back to their original possessors. However, he did not survive for long, and the throne passed to his nephew.

King Tri Ralpachen proved to be a ruler with a passion for art and culture. He is remembered with special veneration because he organized and sponsored a complete revision of all the Buddhist scriptures that had been translated into Tibetan over the previous two centuries. Many of these had been made from secondary sources, such as Kotanese, Chinese, and Kashmiri, and not from the original Sanskrit. As a result, some were accurate and others were not. In addition, they had been made during various periods of scholarship, and thus showed a wide divergence in terminology. He commissioned them all to be reworked by comparing them to the original Sanskrit editions and applying strict guidelines in the usage of terminology and grammar. A special Sanskrit-Tibetan dictionary of technical terms was created for the project, and everyone was expected to adhere to it. Several thousand Buddhist texts were translated or revised under his patronage, and many of these can be found today in the two Tibetan canons: the Kangyur, translated words of Buddha, and the Tangyur, translations of works by later Indian masters.

King Tri Ralpachen was also active in building. His masterpiece was the Onchando Palace, a nine-storied edifice in three tiers.

The first three stories were made of stone, the next three of brick, and the top three of wood. He himself lived in the bottom three; he housed his monks and translators in the middle three; and the top three were reserved for usage as libraries and chapels. Again, as with his predecessors Songtsen Gampo and Trisong Deutsen, many building activities greatly contributed to the Tri Ralpachen's development of the Tibetan artistic tradition.

In 822 he signed a peace treaty with China, the wording of which is relevant to today's China-Tibet situation. A passage of it reads thus:

> The great king of Tibet, a miraculously manifest lord, and the great king of China, the ruler Hvang-ti. . . with the singular desire of bringing peace to their subjects, have agreed upon the higher purpose of ensuring lasting harmony between their two countries. . . .
>
> Between the two nations no smoke nor dust will be allowed to arise. There shall be no sudden incursions, and the very word "enemy" shall not be spoken. . . . The Tibetans will remain with contentment in the land of Tibet, and the Chinese in the land of China. So that this may remain true forever, the Three Precious Jewels and the assembly of saints are invoked as witnesses, as are the sun, moon, planets, and stars.

The treaty was carved into three stone pillars, with one being placed in Lhasa, the second in the Chinese capital, and the third on the border between the two countries.

THE RENAISSANCE OF THE ELEVENTH CENTURY

Not long after Tri Ralpachen's death, the Tibetan empire fragmented, and the Buddhist arts not only lost their state patronage, but even became objects of state persecution, at least in central Tibet. Much of the artwork that had been created over the previous two and a half centuries was destroyed.

However, in the mid-eleventh century the kings of western Tibet, who were centered in Gugey near the Indian/Kashmir border, fostered

Photo credit © TIB

Buddhist scriptures, wrapped in cloth

a renaissance that had far-reaching effects. They sponsored the construction of numerous monasteries, the translation of various important texts, and the execution of a large variety of artworks.

This renaissance took a quantum leap forward in 1042 with the arrival of the Indian master Atisha Dipamkara Shrijnana. His impact on the country was monumental, and set in motion a chain of events that was to revive Buddhism in the country. After his death his chief disciple Lama Drom Tonpa organized and propagated his teachings with tremendous success. The tradition stemming from him is known to history as the Kadam school.

The success of the Kadam movement opened the door for similar movements. Two other very important Buddhist schools were born at this time, the Sakya and Kargyu, both of which were strongly influenced by Atisha's teachings.

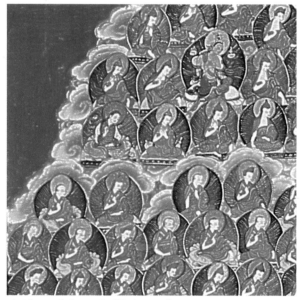
Atisha and the early Kadampa lamas

There is a tendency to speak of "four great schools" and "two periods" of Tibetan Buddhism. When this is done, all the transmissions prior to Atisha are grouped together as the Nyingma, or Old School, and the Kadam, Sakya, and Kargyu are grouped together as the Sarma, or New Schools; the two "periods" become the Old and the New.

Even though Atisha's chief disciple, Lama Drom Tonpa, was not a monk, the Kadam school descending from him quickly became strongly monastic in character. Within a few decades it had swept the country, inspiring the creation of dozens of monasteries throughout Central Asia.

Similarly, both the Sakya and Kargyu schools were founded by nonmonks but soon followed the Kadampa lead and became intensely monastic in character. Thus the new schools that formed in the eleventh century quickly developed large networks of monasteries, with thousands of monks in their organizations. From then until the present day, the monastic model has continued to be extremely popular among Tibetans, with every family wanting to produce at least one monk or nun.

In addition, the lineages coming through Atisha and Lama Drom Tonpa profoundly affected the spiritual character of all schools of Tibetan Buddhism over the centuries to follow, and his doctrines became absorbed by them all. As the present Dalai Lama once said, "Generally we Tibetans do not like the term 'lamaism' that Western scholars use for Tibetan Buddhism, for it seems to imply that our spiritual legacy is something other than the teachings of Buddha. Tibetan Buddhism is simply Indian Buddhism as practiced and developed in Tibet. However, if we were to look for an element that most profoundly characterizes the Buddhism of Central Asia we could say that it is the Kadampa tradition coming from Atisha and Lama Drom Tonpa. Perhaps the word 'lamaism' could be applied to the style of teaching descending from these two masters. It is the lineages from them that have come to serve as the basis of all Tibetan schools of Buddhism."

As we will see in a later chapter, the Kadampas also made a strong contribution to the development of Tibetan art. Most of the building done during the renaissance inspired by Atisha and Lama Drom Tonpa drew from India's renowned Pala style.

Mention should also be made here of a lama from Gugey who became a disciple of Atisha, but who was also a master in his own right. His name was Rinchen Zangpo, and he is known to history as "the Great Translator." He was already famous when Atisha arrived in Tibet, and had inspired the construction of several dozen temples. Many of these still exist in Ladakh, Zanskar, Spitti, and Kinnaur in northwest India. He used artists from Kashmir in his work, and their influence spread eastward with the Kadampa movement that Rinchen Zangpo embraced.

The Mongolian Connection and a New Patron of the Arts

The next important development in Tibetan history, and it carried over strongly into the world of art, was the relationship that grew between the Tibetan lamas and the Mongolian emperors. This relationship became known to

history as *choyon*, or "patron/priest," with the Mongolians serving as patrons of Tibetan Buddhism in return for the Tibetan lamas serving as spiritual preceptors, educators, and tantric priests to the Mongolians.

Mongolia had stepped onto the world's stage as a major power under Genghis Khan, who was born in 1162. By the time Genghis reached his forty-fourth birthday he had brought all eighteen Mongol tribes under his sway and thus was able to proclaim himself emperor of Mongolia. He then conquered the Tartar kingdoms to the north of China, and turned his attention to China itself.

To capture the Chinese empire, he divided his forces into three armies and crossed the Great Wall: the first, commanded by three of his sons, struck from the north; the second, led by his four brothers, entered from the west; and the third, under his own direct command and that of his youngest son, rode in from the northwest. The Chinese forces were no match for his fast-moving horsemen, and soon all of China was his.

Tibet was not spared the expansionist ambitions of Genghis Khan. In 1206 he invaded Tibet and received surrender from the Tibetans in return for granting them nominal autonomy. He had developed a reverence for the Sakya lama Kunga Nyingpo, although he never fully embraced Buddhism. According to the Tibetan account, he sent a letter to Kunga Nyingpo saying that the world was a rough place, and he felt it was his destiny to tame it before turning to the path of Dharma. He died in the effort in 1227.

However, in 1244 his grandson Godan Khan invited Sakya Pandita to the Mongol court.

19

Godan became a Buddhist, and in 1249 conferred rulership of central and western Tibet upon the Sakyas. In 1260, following the death of Godan, Kublai Khan became emperor and extended Sakya authority over all thirteen provinces of Tibet. Thus, following a period of sixteen years of Mongol overlordship, Tibet once more achieved its independence.

Perhaps the most important name in the development of the "patron/priest" relationship between Tibet and Mongolia is that of Sakya Pakpa, the nephew of Sakya Pandita, for he became the guru of Kublai Khan and eventually defined the nature of the choyon arrangement.

Sakya Pakpa was born in 1235 as the great-grandson of Kunga Nyingpo, the head of the Sakya school. From birth he showed all the signs of being a high incarnation, and at the age of eight gave a public discourse to several thousand monks on the *Hevajra-tantra*, one of the highest and most esoteric doctrines taught by the Buddha, and then followed this with an initiation and teaching on the *Kalachakra-tantra*, again one of the most subtle and obtuse Buddhist subjects. It was on this occasion that he was given the name Sakya Pakpa, which means "Arya (i.e., Transcended One) of the Sakya." He dedicated his early years to study and

Early Sakya lamas

meditation, and became renowned as one of the greatest sages of his era.

The West first heard of Kublai Khan's devotion to Sakya Pakpa through the writings of Marco Polo, who visited Kublai's court during this important period. Even though Marco's picture of Sakya Pakpa is somewhat biased (he had been instructed by the Pope to try and introduce Christianity to the Mongols, and naturally resented Sakya Pakpa's presence), his account is nonetheless valuable.

He writes that when he brought up the subject of conversion to Christianity to Kublai Khan, the Khan replied, "Why should I become a Christian? You yourselves must perceive that the Christians of those (Western) countries are ignorant, inefficient people, and do not possess the ability to perform any miraculous deeds. On the other hand, the lamas can easily do whatever they wish in this regard. When I sit at my table the cups in the middle of the hall float to me spontaneously, filled with wine and other drinks, without being lifted by any human hand, and I drink of them. The lamas have many such wonderful powers, and can even control the weather through their rituals. . . . You yourselves have witnessed how their statues are able to speak and to predict the future. . . . Should I convert to Christianity and call myself a Christian, the nobles of my court will ask me why I have done so. They will ask me, 'What extraordinary miracles have been performed by its ministers?' . . .To this I shall not know what to answer, and I shall be considered as having made a grievous error. . . ."

It is possible that Marco's reference to the Tibetan power of telekinesis is an exaggeration, but it nonetheless does say something about the Khan's faith in Tibetan Buddhism and his relationship with Sakya Pakpa.

In return for the spiritual services of the lamas, Kublai Khan gave Tibet its political independence, bestowing upon Sakya Pakpa the title Chogyal, which literally translates as "Dharma King." The nature of the relationship between Tibet and Mongolia that Sakya Pakpa initiated served as the blueprint for a friendship that carried over to relationships with China long after the Mongol rule of China fell to the Ming and then the Manchurians. In fact, it continued almost without interruption until 1911, when the Manchu Dynasty came to an end. During this period the Tibetan lamas acted as the gurus to the Chinese court, in return for which they received immense patronage as well as a guarantee of Tibet's security on the international political scene.

In 1990 the Dalai Lama mentioned an interesting accomplishment of Sakya Pakpa. Apparently, after Kublai Khan consolidated his power over China, he decided to run the country like a labor camp, and felt that there were too many Han Chinese people for the jobs needed to be done, particularly in the field of agriculture. He decided that the population should be

thinned, and to effect this, he would annually have tens of thousands of Han Chinese farmers marched out to the seaside at low tide. When the tide came in they would be washed out to sea and drowned. After he adopted Tibetan Buddhism under Sakya Pakpa, the lama informed him that his method of population control was un-Buddhist and would have to be abandoned.

His Holiness concluded this story by saying, "Thus in the past we Tibetans showed great kindness to the Han Chinese. It is wrong of them to treat us so badly today. Instead, they should be thinking of how to repay this debt that they owe to us."

The Sakya lamas proved to be enlightened rulers of Tibet, and a spirit of religious freedom and tolerance prevailed. All schools of Tibetan Buddhism flourished and evolved during this period. They were great patrons of the arts, and works from their period achieved exceptional sophistication.

Eventually, Sakya rule in Tibet was replaced by that of the Pakmo Drupa, an aristocratic family from Central Tibet, but the choyon relationship with Mongolia and China continued more or less without interruption.

LAMA TSONGKHAPA AND THE SECOND RENAISSANCE

The rule of the Pakmo Drupa kings in the late fourteenth and early fifteenth centuries saw the appearance of a lama of exceptional charisma and genius. This was the famed Lama Tsongkhapa, popularly known to Tibetans as

Gyalwa Nyipa, or the "Second Buddha," who spent years meditating in the Olkha mountains and achieved enlightenment. Tsongkhapa later founded the Gelukpa School, popularly known as the Yellow Hat Tradition due to the yellow pandit hat that their high lamas wear at certain ceremonies. King Jangchub Gyaltsen sponsored the building of Tsongkhapa's Ganden Monastery in 1409, as well as many of his other activities.

Western literature often refers to Tsongkhapa as "the Great Reformer of Tibetan Buddhism," a mistranslation of one of his Tibetan epithets that literally renders as "the Great Reviver of Buddha's Teachings." The mistranslation seems to have its origins in early Western attempts to draw a parallel between Tsongkhapa's work and that of Martin Luther. The comparison is rather ludicrous. Tsongkhapa did not reform Tibetan

Tsongkhapa and his two chief disciples

Buddhism; he studied with fifty-five masters from all the most important spiritual centers of his time and united their teachings into a single lineage. In particular, he took as his foundation the basic approach to Buddhist philosophy and practice that had been outlined by Atisha and the Kadam school, and supplemented this with the tantric lineages from the other traditions, especially the Sakya, Kargyu, Zhalu, and Raluk.

Tsongkhapa's work achieved great success not only due to his personal efforts but also because of the quality of the disciples who were attracted by his eclectic approach. Tens of thousands of students came to him during his teaching career. Five of these, known as his Five Heart-Sons, were supreme, of whom the youngest was Gendun Drubpa, who posthumously became known as the First Dalai Lama.

Tsongkhapa's activities and the tremendous explosion of building activity that it initiated produced an artistic renaissance throughout central Asia. His own commitment to the arts is reflected in a number of events of his life and is listed as one of his four great accomplishments. This is exemplified by his work in repairing the artwork found in many of central Tibet's temples, which at the time were in serious states of dilapidation. Moreover, when he oversaw the creation of the paintings and statues to be housed in the temples and chapels of Ganden Monastery, he took great pains to see that all the most talented artists in the Lhasa area were involved in the project. He did the same when he created the annual Monlam Chenmo, or Great Prayer Festival, in 1410, with King Jangchub Gyaltsen as the chief patron.

The example that he set in this regard inspired a similar commitment to artistic perfection within his disciples. We can see this in the accounts of how Lama Jamyang Chojey built Sera, how Lama Tashi Palden built Drepung, how Lama Jey Sherab Gyatso built Gyumey, and how the First Dalai Lama built Tashi Lhunpo. Their attention to detail and their dedication to artistic excellence shine like glimmering jewels from the pages of their biographies.

The First Two Dalai Lamas

The fifteenth and sixteenth centuries saw a politically unstable period, with numerous Tibetan aristocratic families rising to prominence and then falling. By and large, it could be said that the country was more of a federation of principalities than a nation, with the kings of the different principalities aligning themselves with one another, as well as with various powerful Mongolian tribal chieftains, in order to consolidate the stability of their kingdoms. However, patronage continued to pour in for the construction of temples, monasteries, and meditation hermitages, not only from Tibetan sponsors but also from their Mongolian and Chinese patrons, with the correlative benefits to the world of sacred art.

It was at this point that the Dalai Lamas stepped onto the pages of Tibetan history, and the office of spiritual and temporal leadership fell into their hands.

The First Dalai Lama had been born in 1391 into a family of nomads. His father died when the boy was in his seventh year, and that same year his mother put him in Nartang Monastery under the care of a kindly uncle, Geshey Choshey by name. He quickly impressed the Nartang abbot with his dedication, intelligence, and spiritual sensitivity and became one of the abbot's principal disciples. By his early twenties he had risen to become Nartang's most famous monk. After this he left for central Tibet, where he met with Lama Tsongkhapa four years before the latter's death. He remained in central Tibet

Photo credit © TIB

Looking down on the Oracle Lake

23

for a further decade, studying and meditating with Tsongkhapa's senior disciples, and achieved realization. After this he returned to southwestern Tibet, the land of his birth, where he established Tashi Lhunpo, an institute destined to become southwestern Tibet's most prestigious monastery. He dedicated the remainder of his life to meditating, building, writing, doing teaching tours, and guiding disciples. By the time he passed away in early 1475, he had become one of the most highly revered sages in Central Asia.

Ten months later a child was born with many auspicious signs. As soon as he could speak, he claimed to be the reincarnation of the First Dalai Lama, and not long thereafter was tested by a group of elderly monks from Tashi Lhunpo. Eventually he was recognized and officially enthroned as Gendun Drubpa's reincarnation and was placed in Tashi Lhunpo for training. In his late teens he transferred to Drepung Loseling Monastery near Lhasa, where he completed his education.

Shortly thereafter he met the lama who was to become his main meditation teacher. This was Khedrup Norzang Gyatso, a tantric master who had spent fourteen years in retreat in a cave in the Olkha mountains. The two became inseparable, and in the end the Second Dalai Lama rose to become the principal recipient of all his lineages.

The Second Dalai Lama is remembered for many accomplishments. Two of them became especially important to history: the building of Chokhor Gyal Monastery in the Olkha mountains near the sacred lake Lhamo Latso, together with his empowerment of that site,

which transformed it into a lake of visions that was to be used for prophetic purposes from that time onward; and his creation of a residence, called the Ganden Potrang, for himself and his disciples within the precincts of Drepung Monastery. The visionary lake later also became used as a source of information in the search for the reincarnations of all future Dalai Lamas. Moreover, his future incarnations were in their childhood placed in the Ganden Potrang for education. The Ganden Potrang remained the main residence of the Dalai Lama incarnations, until the Great Fifth built and moved into the Potala in the mid-seventeenth century.

The Second Dalai Lama was in many ways the most important of all the early incarnations in the lineage, for he set the stage for the character and style that the lineage was to assume.

THE DALAI LAMAS BECOME DALAI LAMAS

After the Second Dalai Lama passed away in 1542, a committee was assembled to search for his reincarnation. This was the first time that an official search for a Dalai Lama incarnation was performed, and it was to continue with all future incarnations. Eventually a child was discovered in the Tolung area to the northwest of Lhasa who showed all signs of being the true reincarnation and was installed as such. He became known to history as the Third Dalai Lama.

The child proved to be a natural genius and completed his studies in record time. He became abbot of most of the large monasteries in the Lhasa area, and his fame spread throughout the land.

Meanwhile, the Mongolians, who earlier had embraced Buddhism, had returned to the ways of war. One of their principal chieftains, Altan Khan by name, heard of the Third Dalai Lama's greatness and invited him to teach in the Mongolian court. The master arrived in 1578 and had a monumental impact on the Mongolians. They again took up Buddhist practice and have remained Buddhist and followers of the Dalai Lamas until the present day.

"Dalai" is actually a Mongolian word that first came into use at this time. Previously the lineage was known by the name Tamchey Khyenpa, or "All-Knowing Master." The Third's monastic name was Sonam Gyatso; the second part of this, or "Gyatso," which means "Oceanic," directly translates into Mongolian as Dalai. Thus he became known to the Mongols as the Oceanic Master, or "Dalai Lama." Tibetans themselves never used this name for him to any extent until the present century. However, it became his international title; the Chinese learned it from the Mongolians, and eventually the West learned it from the Chinese.

The Third Dalai Lama spent the remainder of his life traveling and teaching throughout Mongolia, eastern Tibet, and western China. The many monasteries and hermitages that grew in his wake brought a resurgence of sacred art in those regions.

Again, after his death a search committee was established with the responsibility of tracing down his reincarnation. Eventually a child was found in the Mongolian court who passed all tests and eventually was enthroned. The child was directly descended from Genghis Khan, removed from him by nineteen generations.

Even though the Fourth Dalai Lama did not live for long, and passed away in his late twenties, he performed an important function in Central Asian history. The very fact of his ancestry brought a renewed commitment of the Mongolian tribespeople to Tibetan Buddhism, and carried Tibetan art traditions northward at an unprecedented speed. From his time until the present day, the various Mongolian nations have remained cultural satellites of Tibet.

THE GREAT FIFTH

The Fifth Dalai Lama was the first to aquire secular authority. He was born in an unstable period, when the Kargyupa kings of Shigatsey sought to expand their power base. They made a pact with the Bonpo king of Beri, Kham, southeastern Tibet, with the plan to invade central Tibet, destroy the Gelukpa, and divide the spoils between them. Unfortunately for them the plan backfired. Their invasion irritated the Mongolian chieftain Gushri Khan, whose tribe had a large number of children in the Gelukpa monasteries of the Lhasa area. He entered the war, defeated first the king of Beri and then the king of Shigatsey, and brought peace to the land. In 1642 the Fifth Dalai Lama was asked to assume the role of spiritual and temporal leader of Tibet. His reincarnations have retained that role until the present day.

Tibetans refer to the Fifth Dalai Lama as the Great Fifth, for the leadership that he established proved to be very effective and has worked successfully for the Tibetans almost without interruption for the past three and a half centuries, with only a few modifications during the time of the Seventh Dalai Lama.

The Tibetan government took its name from the Fifth Dalai Lama's residence in Drepung (mentioned earlier), the Ganden Potrang, that had been built by the Second. Known as the Ganden Potrang Sizhi Zungtrel, or "The Joyous Seat [working for] Spiritual Peace and Material Prosperity Combined," it devised a system of administration that ushered in a period of prosperity and stability that continued until the Chinese Communist invasion of the 1950s.

In fact, the Dalai Lamas themselves played a very small role in governmental affairs, with the exception of the Fifth and Thirteenth. The Great Fifth set up the structure of the Tibetan government and then retired to a life of meditation, writing, and teaching, leaving the day-to-day workings of the country in the hands of others.

From the Great Fifth until the present Dalai Lama, who is the fourteenth in the line of reincarnations, the Dalai Lama office has remained the principal spiritual and temporal force in Central Asia. The Dalai Lamas have acted as wonderful peacemakers to the Tibetans, guiding them successfully from 1642 until the 1950s through the many challenges that arose. The reign of the Fifth saw the invasion of China by the Manchu tartars, which resulted in the end of the Ming Dynasty and the birth of the Ch'ing; the reign of the Seventh saw the fall of the Mongolians as Asia's foremost power and the rise of the Manchus; and the reign of the Thirteenth saw the decline of the Manchus and the rise of both British and Russian power in Asia. Somehow Tibet under the Dalai Lamas managed to slip through the conflicts without being colonized by any of them. The Manchus managed to gain a foothold in 1728, which they quickly lost, and then again in 1750, which faded within a generation; and both the British and Russians intrigued over Tibet without success during the late nineteenth and early twentieth centuries. When China invaded Tibet in 1950, there were fewer than a hundred foreigners living in the country.

The Great Fifth is remembered for his dedication to the arts and the literary and artistic blossoming that marked his era. His greatest accomplishment, however, was the building of the Potala, one of the world's architectural wonders of the period. All future Dalai Lamas made this building their home.

As Hugh Richardson points out in his wonderful book *Tibet and Its History*, under the Dalai Lamas there was very little distance between the rich and poor in Tibet; famine and abject poverty were almost unknown; and the Tibetans were by and large a happy and contented people with the system they had created.

He points out that the Dalai Lamas owed much of the success of their leadership to the simplicity and directness of the structure that had been implemented by the Fifth and Seventh. Basically they operated with a twofold civil service: a cabinet formed from

Potala Palace, Lhasa

highly trained representatives from aristocratic families; and a religious wing, formed from senior lamas. This ensured that both physical and spiritual issues would be dealt with effectively and humanely. The ordinary citizen had the right of direct appeal to the Dalai Lama whenever he felt that he had been mistreated on any front by a government official.

In many ways Tibet was a federation of a number of kingdoms, united under a common allegiance to the Dalai Lamas, rather than a nation in the modern sense. Most regions maintained their own king or chieftain, as well as local reincarnate lamas that repre-

sented the area. A representative from Lhasa had the role of maintaining the link with them. Politically, the principal role of the Dalai Lama was to ensure that peace was maintained between the different regions, and to bring the people together in times of national emergency. Spiritually, his role was to inspire the regional leaders to patronize spiritual activity in their areas and inspire ordinary citizens to practice the Dharma. In that Tibet prior to the Chinese invasion had an estimated 800,000 monks and nuns and some 6,500 temples, monasteries, and meditation hermitages, he seems to have succeeded quite well in this regard.

RECOGNIZED REINCARNATIONS

The tradition of searching for the reincarnation of a deceased lama was not a legacy unique to the Dalai Lamas, nor was it invented by them. When the Tibetans came into exile in 1959 the country had an estimated three thousand *tulkus*, or officially recognized reincarnates. The procedure of searching for a Dalai Lama reincarnation was more closely supervised than was the search for a lesser lama, but in many ways the process was the same. Essentially it would be reckoned that the spirit of the deceased lama would enter a new womb within a few months, and thus be born within a year of the death of the predecessor. Generally a waiting period of two or three years would be set, so that the child could learn to speak and thus the "tests of speech" could be performed.

During this early waiting period, data would be gathered by a number of means, such as by seeking advice from high lamas and clairvoyants, speaking to oracles, sending a team of experts to meditate beside the Oracle Lake, and so forth. Teams formed from the disciples of the deceased lama would then be sent out to compile a list of names of children born in the areas of the country that had been identified as the probable birthplaces. This list would then be checked by a senior lama, such as the Dalai Lama or (in his minority) one of his gurus, who would perform a divination over it. If the results were positive, the children would be submitted to tests to see which ones showed the most ability to recognize items, people, and so forth from the life of the predecessor. Eventually a child would be recognized as the incarnation and would then be enthroned on the seat of his predecessor, in effect inheriting whatever property the predecessor had left. Usually this would entail a monastery or meditation hermitage, together with whatever land was associated with it. He or she would then be educated in the lineages of the particular institution, and raised to assume the role of leadership.

THE PROPHECY OF THE GREAT THIRTEENTH, AND THE UNFOLDING OF THAT PROPHECY

The Thirteenth Dalai Lama is also often referred to as the Great Thirteenth in Tibetan literature, for, in addition to becoming a great lama, meditator, and Buddhist scholar, he saw Tibet through the critical period that characterized the late nineteenth and early twentieth centuries.

This was the era of "The Great Game," when England and Russia contended for control over Asia, and Tibet became a pawn in their maneuverings. In 1876, the year of the Great Thirteenth's birth, England signed the Chefoo Convention with China, an agreement that in effect gave England a free hand in Burma and Thailand, in return for which China would have a free hand in Tibet, with both signatories having trading rights in both areas. The ploy was masterminded by England in order to steer Tibet away from Russia. Tibet, of course, was not consulted or asked to co-sign on the matter. The Tibetans refused to acknowledge the convention, which led to a British invasion of Tibet in 1888 and again in 1904, followed by a Chinese invasion in 1909. The Great Thirteenth guided Tibet through this dangerous time. In 1913 he expelled all Chinese from Tibet; as for England, he did allow a handful of British diplomats to remain in the country in an advisory capacity, but made clear that their role was solely one of friendship. Tibet remained secure and at peace for the remainder of his life.

He is said to have foreseen the communist invasion of his country and to have attempted to inspire his people to take measures to prevent it. Tibetans tell of how in 1932 the State Oracle spoke of dangers to his life, and of a public sermon that he delivered shortly thereafter. It may be useful to quote a few passages of that sermon.

I have now become rather old, and want to dedicate the remainder of my life to meditation. Unfortunately, it does not look like I will have that luxury. However, I am fifty-eight years old, and soon it will be impossible for me to help much longer. Therefore everyone should look to the future, and think what they can do to contribute themselves.

In particular, we must guard ourselves against the barbaric red communists, who carry misery and destruction with them wherever they go. They are the worst of the worst. Already in Mongolia they have robbed and destroyed the monasteries, forcing the monks to join their armies or else killing them outright. They have destroyed religion wherever they have gone, and even the name of Buddhadharma is not allowed to remain in their wake. . . .

It is not long before we will find this red onslaught at our own front door. It is only a matter of time before we will come into a direct attack from them. If at that time we are not prepared, our spiritual and cultural traditions will be completely destroyed.. Even the names of the Dalai and Panchen Lamas will be erased, as will those of the other lineage masters and holy beings. The monasteries and temples will be looted and destroyed, and the monks and nuns killed or chased away. The great works of the noble and great Dharma kings of old will be undone, all of our cultural and spiritual institutions destroyed, and the birthright and property of our people stolen. We will become like slaves to our conquerors, and will be made to wander helplessly like beggars. Everyone will be forced to live in misery, and the days and nights will pass slowly and with great suffering.

Therefore now, while the strength of peace and happiness is still with us, and the power to act is still in our hands, we should do something about the situation. . . .

You have asked me to give you advice, and therefore I have done so. Please take its essence to heart and think about it day and night. The future is in your hands.

Numerous external rituals have been and are being performed for my long life; but actually the most important thing people can do is follow my advice on this matter.

However, it was not easy to rouse the Tibetans to quick action. They are a traditional and slow-moving people, and the thought of an invasion seemed far off and improbable to them. The Great Thirteenth saw that his advice would not be followed and that the invasion was certain.

It is also said that he had the karma to live until the age of eighty, but understood that if he were to accept this destiny, then he would be an old man at the time of the communist invasion and would be unable to help his people effectively. Therefore he used his meditative power in order to shorten his lifespan, so that when the Chinese invaded there would be a young and vigorous Dalai Lama with whom they would have to contend.

Consequently, the Great Thirteenth died a year after his prophetic sermon, and in July of 1935 a boy was born in a cowshed in the province of Amdo, near the border of Tibet and China, who became recognized as his reincarnation. He was installed as the Fourteenth Dalai Lama in 1939 and prepared for the task that lay before him.

Immediately after Chairman Mao succeeded in ousting the Koumintang and seizing power in China, he announced that he would invade and "liberate" Tibet. Some of his advisers counseled against it, stating that Communist China was still too young and weak to risk incurring the wrath of the West. Mao reportedly stated, "Britain is destroyed by the war, and the Americans are paper tigers. No one will make more than a squeak over the loss of Tibet." His armies rolled into Chamdo in eastern Tibet in 1949, and over the next two years captured the entire country. Hardened by years of war against the Koumintang, and armed with modern weapons supplied to him by the West for his role against Japan, his enormous army had little trouble in crushing Tibetan resistance.

Tibet's art treasures were the first to go. As the Dalai Lama's older brother Taktser Rinpochey once put it, "First they catalogued what was in every temple and monastery, and then systematically pillaged everything. The first wave would collect and carry away the small artworks made of precious metals or jewels. The next wave would carry away things made of semi-precious materials. The third wave would take the next most precious material, such as the silk brocades used to frame the paintings. The fourth wave would carry away statues made of bronze or copper. Like this, they gradually and systematically stole everything from us. In the end only the bare stone walls were left. Then they came with dynamite and leveled these in order to get to the wood used as supports in the structure. In the end only rubble was left."

This was the story with all but a dozen of Tibet's 6,500 cultural institutions. Because libraries were also destroyed, no inventory of what was lost will ever be possible.

The invasion led to the exodus of His Holiness the Dalai Lama and tens of thousands of his followers, who have since that time been living as refugees in India and Nepal, from where they work for the preservation of their culture and their human rights as a people.

In 1989 His Holiness received the Nobel Prize for Peace for the nonviolent policies that characterize his leadership. When once asked why he held to this course so strongly, he replied, "Ours is a civilization that for over a thousand years has been dedicated to nonviolence, compassion, and forgiveness, and therefore we struggle for our rights as a people within the parameters of these principles. If we were to abandon them and regain our land through hatred and violent means, the loss would far outweigh the gain. The Tibet that we would get back would no longer be the Tibet for which we are struggling. We would have an outer victory, but an inner defeat, and would have undermined the very basis of our own identity."

On another occasion he said, "Tibet is now passing through the darkest period in its history. I regard it as a great honor and privilege to be the one to bring it through this ordeal. Perhaps if we can succeed we will not only save ourselves, but also set an important example for other countries on how nonviolence, patience, and reliance upon the power of truth can be the most effective tools in human relations."

He continued, "Mao said that power comes from the barrel of a gun. However, that kind of power has too many terrible side effects. It harms both the winner and the loser in the encounter. Human society has to evolve beyond that approach if we are to survive into the twenty-first century on this little blue planet that we all call home."

❋

Perhaps there is a silver lining in the tragic destruction of Tibet. The late Indologist Prof. A.L. Basham once wrote, "The spread of knowledge of the Tibetan culture in the West within a few decades is in some ways comparable to the spread of knowledge of Greek and classical culture in Europe after the capture of Constantinople by the Turks and the diaspora of Byzantine scholars. It is as though a new dimension has been added to the stock of world civilization. Whereas Tibetan culture was once studied outside of Tibet only by a very few specialists, it is now taught widely in American and European universities and is being studied at various levels all over the world."

The Tibetans have done a good job of preserving their culture as an exiled people living as refugees, and at the same time have made a considerable impact on the international cultural arena.

This exhibit is possible only because of the success of their efforts. In it we try to convey the commitment to gentleness, wisdom, and compassion that has characterized Tibet as a nation for almost fifteen hundred years and is so exquisitely embodied in their artistic traditions.

❋

CHAPTER TWO

THE BUDDHIST LEGACY

Photo credit © TIB

Statue of a Buddha

SIGNIFICANCE OF THE BUDDHA IMAGE

The mystical arts of Tibet are very much linked to the sentiment of enlightenment; a painting or statue is expected not only to embody that sentiment, but also to have the capacity to convey it to the viewer. As the Dalai Lama once put it, "Just by looking at a sacred image we should feel a sense of inner peace and transcendence."

One of the reasons for this is the presence of the 112 major and minor signs of a buddha's body.

The idea is that when someone achieves enlightenment, the mind transforms into the Dharmakaya, or "Truth Body," the emotions transform into the Samboghakaya, or "Beatific Body," and the ordinary body transforms into the Nirmanakaya, or "Emanation Body." Only another buddha can perceive the first of these; aryas, or saints, can perceive the second; and ordinary beings can perceive the third.

The Dharmakaya is formless, and thus cannot be represented by an image. Buddhist artists overcame this obstacle by depicting it as a stupa (see pages 141-2), the different levels of which symbolize the formless wisdom of the Dharmakaya state. It is also sometimes depicted as a simple, unadorned buddha image, the simplicity being used to hint at formlessness.

The Samboghakaya aspect is represented by a Buddha wearing a five-pointed crown, wherein each of the five points signifies one of the five wisdoms (see page 137).

The Nirmanakaya, or "Emanation Body," is the aspect of enlightenment most accessible to ordinary beings. It is characterized by the 112 major and minor marks of perfection, although only people of great merit will be able to perceive these. Statues and paintings of Buddha Shakyamuni are always of this Nirmanakaya aspect. The very fact that he is a historical figure denotes that we are speaking about his visible presence in the world, or Nirmanakaya dimension.

The 112 major and minor marks of perfection are physical attributes that are the product of having cultivated particular spiritual qualities. The Buddhist concept is that our body is the crystallization of our karma; as a being progresses toward enlightenment, his or her karma becomes increasingly refined, and thus the body takes on increasingly refined characteristics. With most beings this is a gradual process of evolution that takes place over a period of many lifetimes; only in the tantric path can it be accomplished in a single lifetime. Among the 112 signs are large earlobes, which signify having listened to many spiritual teachings; clear and strong eyes, which signify having cultivated clear wisdom; wheels on the hands and feet, the result of

having taught the enlightenment path to many beings; and a general beauty of presence, the result of having cultivated the perfection of patience. Each of the signs is given a spiritual explanation along these lines. In that all beings have many links to the spiritual path in one lifetime or another, merely seeing a statue or painting that embodies the 112 marks and signs subliminally arouses a sense of the spiritual qualities being symbolized.

The Tibetan tradition of searching for high reincarnate lamas takes into consideration how many of these 112 marks and signs are clearly visible on the body of the child being tested.

BUDDHA AND THE THOUSAND UNIVERSAL TEACHERS

The etymology of the Sanskrit term "buddha" implies a person who has awakened from the sleep of ignorance and achieved the state of bodhi, or enlightenment. The Tibetans translated bodhi as "jang-joob," with "jang" meaning that the mind is purified of karmic stains and perceptual distortions, and "joob" that it is expanded to an understanding of the two levels of reality, conventional and ultimate.

A Buddhist image should convey this awakened state and the two qualities of purity and expansiveness. The flow of the lines, cast of the eyes, and general presence of the piece should arouse feelings of this nature in the mind of the viewer.

In general, anyone who achieves enlightenment becomes a buddha, and all beings are destined to one day achieve that state. We are all steadily evolving toward it.

In a sense all who achieve buddhahood are equal, for their qualities of love, compassion, wisdom, and so forth have evolved to perfection. However, from the perspective of how they are experienced individually by unenlightened beings, there is a difference, for they all made different karmic connections while training on the enlightenment path. They themselves are not bound by that karma, but it provides them with a special link in communication with the world. The thousand buddhas of this age who have the destiny to serve as universal teachers are special only in that their teaching link with the humans of the era is particularly strong.

Buddha Shakyamuni, who was born 2,500 years ago in Lumbini (located just inside modern-day Nepal near its southwestern border with India), is listed as the fourth such universal teacher of our age. He set in motion a series of teachings that swept across Asia and became, at one point in human history, a source of profound inspiration to over half the world's population. The fifth such "universal teacher" will be Maitreya Buddha (see pages 132-3), who will appear in the future and usher in a golden age.

After achieving his enlightenment, Buddha Shakyamuni taught for forty-five years before passing into parinirvana. Approximately 2,000 texts containing his words exist in translation in the Tibetan canon, or Kangyur; 3,000 texts by the later Indian masters are preserved in the Tibetan Tangyur.

ASPECTS OF BUDDHA SHAKYAMUNI'S TEACHINGS

In the mid-fifteenth century the First Dalai Lama wrote, "The Buddha Shakyamuni taught 84,000 doctrines as a remedy to the 84,000 spiritual distortions. These can be subdivided in various ways. One such way is twofold: the Sutrayana teachings, or Vehicle of Public Discourses; and the Mantrayana teachings, or Vehicle of Secret Mantra Discourses. Another twofold way is into the Hinayana, or Minimalist Vehicle, and the Mahayana, or Universalist Vehicle. Then there is a threefold division: the Shravakayana, or Vehicle of the Listeners teachings; the Pratyekabuddhayana, or Vehicle of the Solitary Realizer teachings; and the Bodhisattvayana, or Vehicle of Bodhisattvas. Another threefold manner is into the Three Turnings of the Wheel of Dharma. However, no matter which structure is used, it should be remembered that with all 84,000 teachings Buddha had but one purpose in mind: to lead trainees of various inclinations and karmic dispositions to the experience of enlightenment. There is no contradiction in any of them when we look at them from this perspective."

The Sutrayana teaching, or Public Discourse Vehicle, is so called because these teachings were taught openly by the buddha and can be practiced openly. The Mantrayana teachings, also called the Vajrayana, or Diamond Vehicle, were taught secretly and are to be practiced in secret.

The Sutrayana in turn has two levels of doctrine: the Hinayana, or Minimalist Vehicle;

and the Mahayana, or Universal Vehicle. The essence of the former vehicle is the practice of what is referred to as the three higher trainings—self-discipline, meditation, and wisdom—in order to achieve personal liberation from suffering and imperfection. The essence of the Mahayana is the practice of the six perfections—generosity, discipline, patience, joyous energy, meditative application, and wisdom—on the basis of the aspiration to achieve full enlightenment in order to be of maximum benefit to all living beings.

The Mahayana is sometimes also spoken of as being twofold: the General Mahayana, which refers to the exoteric Sutrayana teachings; and the Exclusive Mahayana, which refers to the Mantrayana, or esoteric Vajrayana teachings. These are both called Mahayana, because both of them proceed on the motivation of the universal good and both have the same objective of producing full enlightenment as a means of fulfilling the vow of benefiting all sentient beings.

The Mantrayana teachings in turn are divided into four divisions, each of which has numerous individual tantric systems within it. Each of these tantric systems is symbolized by its own principal tantric deity, its own mandala as a symbol of its process, its own "root tantra" text that was spoken by Buddha, and its own system of yoga for accomplishing enlightenment. What differentiates the four levels from one another is the degree to which passionate energy is utilized in the process and the manner in which sexual energy is harnessed. In the fourth and highest level of the tantras, which includes tantric systems such as Guhyasamaja, Heruka Chakrasamvara and Vajrabhairava, so forth (see pages 106-11), the passions are fully tapped.

The essence of tantric practice was expressed as follows by the Seventh Dalai Lama:

> See your body as the temple of a deity,
> View the world as a sacred mandala circle,
> Take all sounds as mystical music, and
> Experience all thoughts as reflections of
> blissful wisdom.

All tantric practice involves two levels of yogic application. On the first of these one cultivates the ego-transformation of viewing oneself and the world as perfect, in conjunction with the clear visualization of the world and its inhabitants as a sacred circle filled with tantric deities. This is done in conjunction with mantra recitation, which reinforces the specific enlightenment qualities symbolized by the individual deity.

Tibetans generally do not practice the second level of yogic application as taught by the three lower tantric divisions. They prefer the second level of highest yoga tantra, which is the fourth and highest division. Here the yogi attempts to "separate" the three levels of the body—gross, subtle, and most subtle—in order to give rise to increasingly transformative levels of consciousness. This is accomplished by gaining control over the subtle bodily energies, or *prana*, loosening the knots in the energy channels and chakras, and causing the breath and heartbeat to subside to the level of ostensible cessation. The state of consciousness that then arises is such that thereafter the power of a day of meditation becomes equal to that of a hundred years of meditation on the basis of an ordinary mind. For this reason, tantra is often called "the fast path."

THE THREE TURNINGS OF THE WHEEL OF DHARMA

As mentioned above by the First Dalai Lama, there is also a tradition of speaking about Buddha's "Three Turnings of the Wheel of Dharma." This is done from the perspective of both the philosophical content of the doctrine and its practice.

Here the "first turning" refers to Buddha's early teachings, wherein he taught the four aspects of being as understood by the aryas, or the four noble truths: how unenlightened existence is fraught with dissatisfaction and suffering; how these undesirable states have their causes, which are twofold, namely, behavioral patterns and distorted mental states; how there are states of happiness and freedom that are beyond dissatisfaction and suffering; and how these also have their causes. This fourth factor, which is also known as the noble truth of the path, refers to the eightfold path as understood by the aryas: correct action, correct effort, correct livelihood, correct meditation, correct wisdom, and so forth.

Philosophically speaking, the essence of this "first turning of the Dharma wheel" is the doctrine of how all things arise in dependence on the wheel of interdependent arising and co-exis-

tence. Its focus is the doctrine of the egolessness of the person, or the beyond-self-nature of being. This aspect of Buddha's teaching is associated with the Hinayana, or Minimalist Vehicle.

The "second turning" refers to Buddha's teachings at Vulture's Peak, wherein philosophically he explicitly outlined the doctrine of emptiness, or the Great Void, with emphasis not on the beyond-self-nature of the person, but on the void nature of all things. From the side of practice, the emphasis is on the Mahayana bodhisattva trainings, such as cultivation of the mind of universal responsibility, the training in the six perfections, and so forth.

The "third turning" philosophically resolved points of doubt opened up by the first two turnings, with the emphasis being on the mind-only doctrine i.e., how objects of experience are of one and the same nature as the experiencing mind. On the practice side, the emphasis is on the Mahayana bodhisattva trainings.

Thus the first turning of the Dharma wheel is linked to the Hinayana, and the second and third turnings to the Mahayana. As for the secret Mantrayana, it has links to both the second and third turnings.

The above structures of Buddha's teachings were developed by the Indian masters and appear in Indian literature from the second century A.D. onward. The Tibetans absorbed these approaches from the Indians, but preferred to structure the 84,000 teachings somewhat differently, into the threefold category of Hinayana, Mahayana, and Mantrayana doctrines. This did not mean that they were adding something to Buddha's original teachings or leaving anything out, as some Western scholars have suggested, but simply that they found this arrangement more practical.

It works well historically. The teachings of the first turning, or Hinayana doctrines, were widely propagated in the early period of Buddhism in India. They were the form of Buddhism patronized by Emperor Ashoka in the third century B.C. and thus became the most widespread. The general Mahayana doctrines began to be more widely propagated from about the first century A.D. onward, largely because to the work of the Indian master Nagarjuna. The Mantrayana, or tantric teachings, began to become widespread in India from approximately the fourth or fifth centuries A.D.

Because these three levels of Buddhist doctrine surfaced in this sequential order, many Western scholars feel that the "first turning" teachings are original and authentic teachings of the Buddha, while the General Mahayana and Mantrayana teachings are the creations of later Buddhist masters.

The Tibetans do not agree. Their understanding is that the Buddha taught all three—Hinayana, Mahayana, and Mantrayana—and that these merely surfaced and achieved widespread popularity in a sequential order. The Mahayana and Mantrayana were taught more secretly in the early days, and became openly propagated only when the times were ripe for them.

Be this as it may, by the time Buddhism began to make strong inroads into Tibet, all three were publicly known in India, and there was a tendency to see them as noncontradicto-ry, with the Hinayana being used as the initial training, the General Mahayana as the intermediate training, and the Mantrayana as the advanced practice.

HEROES OF THE ENLIGHTENMENT PATH

Each of the three vehicles—Hinayana, Mahayana, and Mantrayana—has its own heroic personality, or role model. That of the Hinayana is the arhat, the retired, gentle, saintly sage who has achieved the state of individual nirvana; that of the Mahayana is the bodhisattva, who takes the vow of universal responsibility and works to achieve the full enlightenment of buddhahood as the best means of benefiting all sentient beings; and the hero of the Mantrayana is the mahasiddha, the tantric yogi or yogini who usually is eccentric in personality and magical in action. The mahasiddha achieves the same buddhahood as the bodhisattva, but does so with a more unconventional flare. We see all three of these personalities depicted in the Lama Chopa Assembly Tree (see pages 122-3).

A saying by the early Kadampa masters sums up the Tibetan approach to how the three are to be integrated into a single practice:

> Externally practice the gentle ways of the
> shravakas
> [i.e., the Hinayana, or way of the
> arhat];
> Internally practice the bodhisattva
> perspective

[i.e., the Mahayana, or way of the bodhisattva];
And secretly practice the way of secret mantra
[i.e., the Mantrayana, or way of the mahasiddha].

Tibetan Lineages of Buddhist Practice

As mentioned earlier, the Buddha's teachings came to Tibet in two major waves: the earlier wave, which include all transmissions that occurred prior to the eleventh century, and are grouped together as the Nyingma, or Old School; and the later wave which developed in the eleventh and twelfth centuries, the movements which are known as the Sarma, or New Schools. The Kadam, Sakya, and Kargyu were the major New Schools to emerge in the eleventh century. In that the Kadam became the basis of and was absorbed by the Gelukpa School in the late fourteenth and early fifteenth centuries, the Gelukpa is also counted as among the Sarma, or New Schools.

There is also a tradition of speaking of the Yellow Hat and the Red Hat schools of Tibetan Buddhism. When this is done, the "Yellow Hats" refers to the Gelukpa; everyone else is grouped together as "Red Hat" schools. This is because prior to Lama Tsongkhapa's time all lamas wore a red pandit hat on ceremonial occasions; Tsongkhapa introduced a yellow hat for his school, because yellow allegedly was the color worn

by the masters of early Indian Buddhism, and he wanted to signify a return to the basic roots of Buddhism.

Even though each school of Tibetan Buddhism has its own individual character and style, as well as minor philosophical differences, they all are combinations of the sutra and tantra teachings of the Buddha. Each combines the Hinayana, Mahayana, and Mantrayana practices and sees the first two as preliminaries to the third, while regarding the third as being the highest and most powerful.

As the Dalai Lama put it, the differences between the Tibetan Buddhist schools are more of a historical, geographical, and linguistic nature. Each developed in a different period of Tibetan history, or in a different region of the country. As a result, they have slightly different usages of linguistics and terminology.

In terms of practice, all four major schools are similar in that they all advocate cultivating spiritual detachment by meditating on the four noble truths, maintaining inner purity by following the noble eightfold path, generating the bodhisattva attitude of universal responsibility through meditation on love and compassion, and arousing wisdom by maintaining awareness of how emptiness and conventional reality co-exist within every phenomenon. All four schools regard these trainings as prerequisites to entering into tantric practice and suggest that after gaining maturity in them, we receive tantric initiation into a mandala and then maintain the tantric precepts. All four teach the two levels of tantric training: the generation stage, in which ego-transformation

Photo credit © TIB

Meeting of Heaven and Earth

through identification with the mandala deity is cultivated, in conjunction with meditation on the world as mandala, and mantra recitation; and they all teach the completion stage, with the yogas for separating the subtle vajra body through meditation on the vital energies, the chakras, and so forth.

In the final analysis, there is usually more difference between how any two lamas from the same school teach their disciples than there is between the sects in general, because of the individualistic nature of the Tibetan teaching style. As the Tibetan saying goes, "Each lama is his own sect."

The destruction of Tibet by the Chinese Communist invasion has meant the loss of many of the smaller lineages of transmission. However, the main body of the teachings preserved in the four main schools has been preserved in the refugee community in India and Nepal under the guidance and supervision of His Holiness the Dalai Lama.

❀

CHAPTER THREE

THE NATURE OF TIBETAN SACRED ART

Photo credit © TIB

Wall painting in the Potala

THE BACKGROUND

The art of a people develops in relationship to a particular background. This being the case, we can surmise that the sacred art of Tibet grew out of the three periods of the country's own cultural unfolding, which were discussed in Chapter One: the aboriginal period of the Lopa tribes, which had an art similar to that of our own North American natives; the Bonpo period, which absorbed elements from the kingdom of Tazig, or Persia, the source of its new religion; and the Buddhist period, which began with King Songtsen Gampo in the mid-seventh century and kicked into high gear a hundred years later with King Trisong Deutsen.

Our exhibit focuses on the third of these, the Buddhist period, because this is the art form that came to dominate the Land of Snows.

Again, the development of Buddhist art in Tibet reflects the manner in which Buddhism came to that country. During King Songtsen Gampo's time, monks from half a dozen areas traveled and taught in several regions in and around Tibet, principally (1) Magadha, or north/central India; (2) the Newari regions of Nepal's Kathmandu Valley; (3) Kashmir; (4) Oddiyana, or modern-day northeast Pakistan; (5) Khotan, a now-extinct oasis kingdom to the northwest of Tibet on the Silk Route; and (6) China, Tibet's important neighbor to the east. The accounts of the construction during King Songtsen Gampo's reign of the Jokang and Ramochey temples, as well as the 108 minor spiritual centers, mention artisans being brought in from all these areas. Because Songtsen Gampo ruled large parts of all of them, this was easy enough for him to arrange. Similarly, when King Trisong Deutsen a hundred years later commissioned the building of Samyey, Tibet's first monastery, we again see the names of artists from these six countries being mentioned.

India, of course, was the principal source of inspiration for all Buddhist art, because it was the land of Buddha's birth and where Buddhism first flourished. The artistic traditions that developed in India during the spread of Buddhism in that country provided the launching ground from which all other countries later embarked upon their individual Buddhist artistic adventures.

THE FIRST BUDDHIST IMAGES

Buddhist legend claims that a number of images of the Buddha were fashioned during his actual lifetime. Western scholarship takes a different view, and holds that in the early days of Buddhist history only the stupa, or memorial reliquary (see page 144), was used; they claim that the tradition of making paintings and statues of the Buddha came much later, only after contact with the Greeks. There is no need here to go into the reasoning behind this theory. Instead we will look at the history of the Buddha image as presented in the original Tibetan texts.

The first image of the Buddha is said to have been a painting, and is known in Tibetan as *Chu-len-ma*, which translates as "Taken from Water. " According to the traditional account, it was commissioned by King Bimbisara, one of Buddha's great supporters. The legend states that King Bimbisara had received a priceless gem as a gift from a neighboring monarch, King Utayana, and wanted to send back something of equal splendor in return. He came up with the idea of commissioning a portrait of the Buddha for this purpose, and requested the Buddha for his permission.

The Buddha agreed to sit in order to be painted, and King Bimbisara set his greatest artists to the task. However, they were so overwhelmed by the Buddha's radiant and sublime presence that they were unable to look directly at him. Buddha therefore led them to a nearby pool of water, and suggested that they paint the reflection that appeared in it. The artists studied the reflection carefully, taking the measurements that have continued to be used over succeeding centuries as the icnographical guidelines for creating a buddha figure (see page 55). Buddha suggested that the image be surrounded by a circle containing symbolic images representing the twelve links of interdependent origination. King Bimbisara sent the painting to King Utayana, who eventually achieved sainthood by means of meditating upon it.

Another image made during the Buddha's lifetime is known as *Tubpa Odzerma*, or "The Image Taken from Light-rays." The story here is that King Mahanama's queen had a maidservant by the name of Rohita. When the Buddha was passing through their kingdom, the queen sent Rohita to deliver an offering to him. However, Rohita was killed on the way by bandits. She was reborn as a princess in a kingdom to the south of India, and as a youth heard of and developed great devotion to the Buddha. She sent a letter with an offering to him, and the Buddha wrote back to her in order to express his gratitude, enclosing with the letter a portrait of himself. This image had been created by having the Buddha project his aura onto a canvas, the design of which the artists then filled in with color. This image so inspired the princess that she achieved realization through her devotions to it.

Several statues of the Buddha are also said to have been made during his lifetime. Tibetan scriptures relate that the Buddha once accepted to have the renowned Indian artist Bhavakrama create three different images of him: the first of him in the form of an eight-year old boy; the second as a twelve-year old; and the third as a young man of twenty-five. The first eventually ended up in China, the second in Nepal, and the third in Devaloka.

Another statue said to have been created during the Buddha's lifetime was made of sandalwood and depicts him in the standing position. This image reportedly was later taken to China, and to have inspired the widespread Chinese tradition of the standing Buddha figure.

Also, the wealthy businessman Anathapindika, Buddha's greatest patron, is said to have commissioned a statue of the Buddha that was precise in every detail, and was made of precious gems.

In addition, tradition states that the Buddha's own son Rahula commissioned a statue of his father. Made of precious stones and gems, it presented the Buddha as Rahula had seen him. Because of the materials from which it was made, Tibetans refer to it as *Rinchen Tonpa*, or "The Jewel Master."

Tibetan histories state that immediately after the Buddha's death Buddhist temples were constructed in India, with the images of the Buddha being created for them. For example, one family of statue-makers is said to have constructed three important images. The eldest brother, Jina by name, fashioned a statue from semi-precious stone for a temple in Sarnath. The middle brother, Sadhujina, had clay brought from the eight Buddhist holy places and used it to make a statue for a temple in Rajgir. Finally, the youngest brother, Kushala, created a statue depicting Buddha at the moment of his enlightenment for a temple at Bodh Gaya.

Immediately after the Buddha's death and cremation, his ashes and relics were divided equally between the eight main clans of his patrons and followers. The recipients carried these precious substances to their homelands and had stupas created in order to house them. Monasteries quickly built up around these stupas, with Buddha images being created for their temples.

The Tibetans claim that these early paintings and statues, created during the Buddha's lifetime or immediately after his death, served as the basis from which all Buddhist art is descended.

LATER DEVELOPMENTS IN INDIA

All the images made during these formative years (an exception, according to Tibetan myth, is one of the images brought to Tibet by King Songtsen Gampo's Chinese wife) were lost to the ravages of time. The paintings were made on perishable materials and were the first to go. As for the statues, these were made either of precious gems or sandalwood, both of which have short lives, the former because of thieves and the latter because of the fragility of the material and the effect that a tropical climate has upon them.

Nonetheless, many Indian artworks from later generations have survived. The most numerous are in the category of large stone statues and carved temples, as well as several exquisite cave paintings, but these are from later periods. Today the remnants of these stone images fill the museums of India, Pakistan, and various cities in the West. The cave paintings can be found in Ajanta and Elmora in South India. The ruins of several carved temples, such as that at Sanchi, still remain.

In brief, India's contribution to the world of Buddhist art can be seen in the Gupta-style art from the Agra area, Gandhara-style pieces from Pakistan and Afghanistan, and Pala-style images from East India. The hundreds of pieces surviving in whole or as fragments all bear testimony to the fervor of artistic activity that took place in the land of the Buddha's birth long before the Muslim invasions of that country resulted in the destruction of India's great Buddhist centers.

Certainly India's sophistication in the Buddhist arts was already highly developed when Buddhism began to flow into Tibet under King Songtsen Gampo's reign in the mid-seventh century, and had spread to Nepal, Kashmir, Pakistan, Afghanistan, Khotan, and China long before that time.

FROM IMPORTED TO INDIGENOUS TRENDS IN TIBETAN ART

In *Tibetan Painted Scrolls* Prof. Tucci mentions three important stages in the formative period of Tibet's Buddhist art. First there was the era of the Three Dharma Kings, from the mid-seventh to early ninth centuries, when Buddhism came to Tibet under royal patronage and experienced a whirlwind of building activity. Here the Indo-Nepali and Chinese schools provided the strongest influences, but artists from various other neighboring countries, as mentioned earlier, also participated. After the great debate between the Indian and Chinese schools in 792, Chinese influences waned, and the Indo-Nepali style predominated.

The second important development period was inspired by the advent of the Indian master Atisha in 1042 and the early Kadampa movement that followed in his wake. In the early days this movement achieved its greatest success in western and central Tibet and drew most heavily from Kashmiri influences, as well as from the Pala style of India that flowed into Tibet via Nepal.

Detail from tangka page 113

Third, the rise of the Sakya sect to a role of political dominance in the thirteenth century, which was described earlier, initiated a trend that was to set the tone for future developments in Tibetan art. The principal Sakya monastery was located in Tsang, not far from the Nepal border, and thus artistically drew strongly from the classical Indo-Nepali tradition, which was characterized by a minimalist background and perspective. However, the fact that the Sakya

lamas served as spiritual advisers and educators to the Mongolian emperors of China also brought a strong influence from the Chinese styles of the day, which showed a unique attention to perspective and background. Even though Tibetan art during the seventh, eighth, and ninth centuries had taken directions from the traditions of these two countries, it was now four hundred years later, and the arts from which they were drawing had been transformed considerably. The marriage of the two styles, coupled with innovations from the unique Tibetan genius, launched what may be called the beginning of an indigenous national Tibetan style, for Sakya influence during this period extended over the entire land. As Pratadaditya Pal points out in *Tibetan Paintings*, the wealth that poured into Sakya coffers as a result of royal Mongol patronage, combined with the Sakya devotion to art, inspired Tibet's painters and sculptors to a new level of excellence.

THE MENTRI, NEW MENTRI, AND GADRI STYLES

In mid-fifteenth century a Tibetan artist came on the scene who achieved such national prominence that he might correctly be called the forefather of a truly indigenous Tibetan style of painting. His name was Menla Dondup, and in many respects he stands as the Michelangelo of the Tibetan art world. He gathered together the various strands of Buddhist art extant in the Land of Snows, wove them together, and revised them into a style that is known to history as the Mentri school or "Images of Menla." In addition, he developed various pigments and approaches to color that soon became emulated by artists throughout the length and breadth of Tibet. The innovations that he established have continued over the 550 years since his advent, and are still the most commonly used techniques adopted by Tibetan artists today. When Prof. Tucci in *Tibetan Painted Scrolls* states that a singular character can be seen in Tibetan paintings throughout Central Asia, from Ladakh on the west to China on the east, and from Siberia on the north to the borders of Nepal on the south, this "singularity of character" can be accredited to Menla Dondup.

Tibetan texts on art history mention an Old Mentri school and a New Mentri school. The former dates to Menla Dondup himself, whereas the latter dates to the mid-seventeenth century and a man known as Choying Gyatso. The New Mentri school is based on the Old, but is characterized by new developments in pigment technology, as well as a tendency to incorporate a slightly more Chinese approach to perspective. The New Mentri school achieved national attention and a lasting impact because it was patronized by both the Fifth Dalai Lama, who became spiritual leader of Central Asia and temporal ruler of Tibet in 1642, and also his guru, the First Panchen Lama. Both of these lamas were great patrons of the arts, and their preference for the New Mentri School ensured a national popularity for the style.

Some Tibetan art histories mention a third school, the Karma Gadri, which developed in eastern Tibet in the sixteenth century and is based on the work of an artist by the name of Namkha Tashi. However, although this movement produced numerous works of rare beauty, it never achieved national prominence. In a sense it was not a truly indigenous Tibetan style, but rather an extension of Ming Chinese art, with a few Tibetan overtones.

Most Tibetan artists today follow an approach to painting that is a combination of the Old and New Mentri schools.

THE STATUE-MAKERS

What has been said above mostly is in reference to Tibetan painting styles. The development of Tibetan statue-making largely followed the same pattern of development, although here throughout its history Tibet has most closely followed the Indo-Nepali styles that they learned from the Newari Buddhist artists of the Kathmandu Valley, especially in the realm of metalwork and casting. The Newaris have since the earliest of times until the present day produced statue-makers and metalwork artists of the highest caliber to be found in Asia. In the following chapter we will look at some of the techniques incorporated in this important field of Tibetan mystical art.

CHAPTER FOUR:

THEMES OF TIBETAN SACRED ART

Rock painting

Photo credit © TIB

THE POWER OF SACRED IMAGES

Tibetan sacred paintings and statues focus on a large number of subjects. Most of these are what can loosely be described as "divinities," or what Tibetans call *lha*. These "divinities" belong to various categories, and are perhaps best illustrated by one of our paintings, the Lama Chopa Assembly Tree (see page 123).

The Tibetan word for a sacred image is *ten*, which translates as "support." The idea is that the physical image acts as a base that can support or encourage the presence of the divinity being portrayed. After a painting or statue is completed, it will be consecrated, and the blessings of the forces of goodness brought into it. The forces thus invoked and channeled into the image are known in Tibetan as *tenpa*, or "the supported." Only when the consecration ceremony has been completed does the image become sacred.

There are three forms of the consecration ritual: short, medium, and extensive. The short form takes only a few moments to perform; the medium version requires a complete day; and the extensive version takes three days. In extensive consecration rituals many monks will chant and meditate over the objects from dawn to dusk during the three-day period. The Dalai Lama and the hundred monks of his private monastery perform this extensive consecration ceremony every year. Tibetans and other Buddhists from around the world send their newly made images to his temple in Dharamsala to have them placed in his temple during this period.

There is also a deconsecration ritual, which is performed if a work is to be restored or renovated, and also when a damaged work is to be destroyed.

Tibetans believe that a consecrated image acquires and embodies paranormal abilities and is able to speak to people of great merit, deliver prophecies, physically move about, and so forth. They did not invent this belief, but rather inherited it from the Indian masters.

For example, when Atisha received an invitation in the early eleventh century to come and teach the Dharma in Tibet, he went for a walk and circumambulated the great stupa in Bodh Gaya to think the matter over. The stupa contained a number of images of the buddhas and bodhisattvas, including one especially holy image of the female bodhisattva Arya Tara. He paused in front of this image and prayed for guidance. The image spoke to him, saying that to go to Tibet would greatly shorten his lifespan but would be of tremendous benefit to sentient beings and Dharma in the long run. Consequently, he accepted the invitation; his work in Tibet achieved such success that today his lineages serve as the singularly most unifying force in all the schools of Tibetan Buddhism.

There are many such stories of the Indian masters receiving advice and prophecies directly from statues and paintings. The Tibetans continued this legacy. Most Tibetan monasteries contained at least one image that was believed to exhibit this power frequently.

When Tsongkhapa led the first celebration of the Great Prayer Festival in Lhasa in 1410 the main Buddha image in the Jokhang Temple is said to have spoken to him and delivered numerous prophecies. Similarly, during the festival of 1959, a few months before the tens of thousands of Tibetans were forced into exile, it is said to have shed tears in the presence of hundreds of people.

THE SUBJECTS OF TIBETAN SACRED ART

As said earlier, Tibetan Buddhism is a combination of the Sutrayana and Mantrayana, or exoteric and esoteric aspects of the teachings of Buddha. The concept of "divinity" is used quite differently in these two fields, so it may be useful to look at what is said in both.

Art works associated with the Sutrayana tradition mostly include images in the following categories: buddhas, arya bodhisattvas, arhats, lineage masters, and/or worldly gods. Let's look at each of these categories and their meaning in the Sutrayana teaching.

The buddhas are the beings who have achieved enlightenment. The buddha most commonly depicted in Sutrayana art is Buddha Shakyamuni (see pages 92-93), the historical figure who established the enlightenment tradition in the present world age. The sutras mention Buddha Shakyamuni as the fourth such universal teacher of this world cycle, and as the seventh in recorded history (the four of this age, plus three from the previous world age). These are known as "the Seven Buddhas of Recorded History." In addition, there is the prophesied Buddha Maitreya, who will be the fifth universal teacher of our age. In addition, the Mahayana sutras introduce a number of other buddhas, such as Amitabha, who are presented as lords of mystical paradises, into which devotees can take rebirth. Then there are the buddhas of the three times and ten directions, who represent all the nameless beings who have and will achieve enlightenment, and the "Thirty-five Buddhas of Confession," who are the objects of devotion in a liturgy for purifying the mind of negative karma.

In the Sutrayana tradition the buddhas are usually depicted as monks with their bodies adorned with the 112 major and minor marks of perfection. Hence they all look more or less identical and can be distinguished as individuals only by their hand positions and the objects that they hold.

Second are the arya bodhisattvas, or "sacred warriors." All beings who have taken the vow of universal responsibility are known as bodhisattvas, and all buddhas are also bodhisattvas. The arya bodhisattvas are those who have achieved realization of the great void in their meditations. The Hinayana sutras list as bodhisattvas only the Buddha in his previous lives and Maitreya. The Mahayana sutras, on the other hand, list hundreds of bodhisattvas, eight of whom are known as "the eight close spiritual heirs of the Buddha." These eight include Avalokiteshvara (who is depicted on our cover), Manjushri, and so forth. Many bodhisattvas are female, such as Arya Tara.

The arhats are the disciples of Buddha who achieved nirvana. A buddha is also an arhat, as are many bodhisattvas. Iconographically the arhats are usually depicted as serene and gentle monks.

Sutrayana art also includes a number of worldly divinities. These include the Hindu gods, and also the four directional protectors. Buddhism does not accept worldly gods as ultimate objects of refuge, regarding them as highly evolved yet still unenlightened; however, it does respect them as great beings who can be worshipped for worldly purposes, such as health and wealth. Several of them, usually Indra, Brahma, and the four directional protectors, are often depicted in paintings as sitting or standing below the Buddha and making offerings to him (see page 93). According to legend, after Siddhartha the prince renounced his kingdom and became Gotama the monk, the four directional protectors appeared and offered him a begging bowl. Similarly, after Gotama achieved enlightenment and became the Buddha, the god Indra appeared and requested him to teach the Dharma.

Making or keeping a sacred image of any of the above holy beings is said to be a source of great merit and blessing. In addition, it acts as a reminder of the spiritual path and inspires the owner of the image to maintain awareness of meditation and the spiritual qualities.

Tantric Images

The Mantrayana, which is also known as the Vajrayana and the Tantrayana, incorporates a far larger number of deities. In addition to those used in the Sutrayana, it speaks of "the meditational deities of the four classes of tantras," and also of the dakas, dakinis, and dharmapalas.

Technically speaking, the meditational deities, or *Yidam* in Tibetan, are forms of the buddhas. Each meditational deity has its own mandala, as well as its own cycle of tantric texts upon which its practice is based, and each represents a specific path to enlightenment. Each of the four levels of tantra has a large number of meditational deities, and thus of mandalas. In general, those of the fourth and highest level are depicted as wrathful and lusty, because they use the passions of anger and desire as the path to enlightenment. The meditational deities of the three lower tantric classes are generally depicted as more gentle and passive.

The dakas and dakinis, which literally translate as "space travelers," i.e., angels and angelettes, are of two types: worldly and enlightened. The latter are also meditational deities, and the most popular in this category with Tibetans is probably Vajrayogini (see page 125). The worldly class of dakas and dakinis is rarely depicted in Tibetan art, whereas the enlightened class of them is a popular subject.

The dharmapalas similarly include both enlightened and worldly deities. The enlightened dharmapalas usually are Indian in origin.

They represent popular gods and spirits that were sworn to the protection of the Buddhist tradition in India, and thus were practiced by the Indian mahasiddhas. Generally they are thought of as being "activity emanations" of the Yidams, and thus are actually buddhas disguised as simple protectors. They usually are depicted as being extremely wrathful in appearance, for their function is that of "tough love," i.e., to forcefully remove obstacles to the life and spiritual practice of the initiate. Examples are Mahakala, Dharmaraja (see page 111), and so forth. There are also a number of converted Tibetan gods who are regarded as enlightened dharmapalas, but these are rare and are almost never propitiated outside the sect that initiated their usage.

Worldly dharmapalas, on the other hand, are almost always gods of non-Buddhist traditions that became incorporated into Buddhism by means of a ritual called "binding," meaning that a tantric master once ritually bound them to the service of enlightenment, thus gaining from them an oath to work for the protection of spiritual practitioners. In that Central Asia was very much a conglomerate of shamanic traditions before the advent of Buddhism, its many valley and mountain gods were soon "bound to service" by the early tantric masters. Guru Padma Sambhava himself is said to have done this with many of the Bonpo gods when he came to Tibet in the mid-eighth century. Most Tibetans still maintain a devotional practice focusing on a traditional family protector, which includes a daily incense offering and a monthly invocation. The liturgies to these deities is always preceded by an invocation of the Yidam, or Buddhist meditational deity, to symbolize that the ancient shamanic tradition has been sublimated by the Buddhist process.

DIMENSIONS OF THE DIVINITY

Tibetans speak of all these spiritual figures in various ways. One of them is the threefold division of outer, inner, and secret.

For example, if we consider Avalokiteshvara, the Bodhisattva of Compassion, the outer interpretation is that he is a being who once was an ordinary being like us. He then embarked upon the path to enlightenment, with compassion as the spearhead of his practice, and became an example of the profound powers of compassion. His deeds of compassion achieved such renown that he came to be regarded as the foremost embodiment of compassion in action. Thus, in this interpretation, Avalokiteshvara is an actual spiritual being with a biography and history.

The inner interpretation is that Avalokiteshvara is a symbol of compassion and its attributes, a spiritual quality that we all possess in latent form. The palms of his two hands are folded together in the mudra of compassion; between them he holds a wish-fulfilling gem, for the practice of compassion fulfills all wishes for oneself and others. When he is depicted with four hands, the four represent love, compassion, the ability to always experience joy at the success of others, and the equanimity that holds compassion for all others regardless of their so-called worthiness. Sometimes he is depicted with a thousand hands and eyes, for compassion works to benefit the world in a thousand ways, and watches with a thousand eyes of wisdom.

Secretly, Avalokiteshvara represents the manner in which the spiritual quality of compassion is always present in every experience, and we can learn to extract it. The most harsh and painful ordeal can be a teacher of compassion.

This threefold dimension of the bodhisattva Avalokiteshvara is common to both Sutrayana and Mantrayana interpretations. In addition, the Mantrayana utilizes Avalokiteshvara not merely as an object of devotion and a symbol of compassionate energy, but as a mandala deity that is a symbol of a yogic path to enlightenment, meditation upon which can bring compassionate wisdom to fulfillment and invoke the experience of full enlightenment in one lifetime.

Similarly, the outer picture of the symbolism of Manjushri, the Buddha of Wisdom, is that of a being who was once an ordinary being but who embarked upon the path to enlightenment; he took the development of wisdom as the spearhead of his spiritual practice, and eventually accomplished the extraordinary state of buddhahood. The inner interpretation is that Manjushri represents or symbolizes the wisdom that lies dormant within all of us and can be awakened. Secretly, he embodies the manner in which a wisdom message is hidden in all experiences.

Buddhists keeping an Avalokiteshvara or Manjushri image in their home are reminded of these three qualities. Externally, they expect to receive the blessings of that bodhisattva divinity; internally, they hope to achieve inspiration in the cultivation of their own inner quality of compassion and wisdom; and secretly, they hope to become more open to the qualities of compassion and wisdom that are woven into the experience of the world.

DIVINITIES AS TANTRIC MEDITATIONAL DEITIES

In the Mantrayana both Avalokiteshvara and Manjushri become Yidams, or meditational deities. This means that in addition to the above threefold interpretation, they also become embodiments of an elaborate yogic process that generally is divided into two stages of tantric application: the yoga of symbols, which is also known as the yoga of creative imagination; and the yoga beyond symbols, in which the real meaning of the divinity is invoked.

In the first of these two stages the meditator contemplates how his or her own true nature is one with the qualities of the deity; this is also known as the yoga of ego reidentification, or the yoga of divine ego. The world and all that appears in it is dissolved into light, to symbolize how one's own true nature is pure luminosity; and then from within the light one visualizes that one arises as the mandala deity, with the world as a sacred residence and all other living beings as divine beings. This cuts off the ordinary sense of self, uses one's natural egotism as a force for transformation, and eliminates the mundane habitual manner of experiencing the world. One then engages in the mantra recitation, which reinforces within oneself and the world the sacred qualities symbolized by the deity.

In the second stage of yogic application the meditator dispenses with the symbolic process and instead engages directly in *shamatha* combined with *vipassyana*, which means formless meditation in which the way things appear and the beyond-appearance nature of things are taken as the object of contemplation. The focus is the deeper nature of the mind and its luminosity, which is the ultimate deity.

SYMBOLS AND SYMBOLISM

In addition to these various "divinity forms" used as subjects of Buddhist sacred art, a richness in natural symbolism is incorporated. For example, lotus flowers abound to symbolize the natural beauty and purity of the spiritual process. The deities sit on seats made of a lotus, a sun and a moon, with the lotus representing purity, the sun the female quality of wisdom, and the moon the male quality of energy/compassion.

Paintings always try to incorporate images representing the balance of the natural elements. We see earth, water, sky, and clouds, to demonstrate how in the spiritual process our experience of the world enters into a sphere of balance and harmony. Often birds or wild animals are seen in the background to show how the spiritual practitioner achieves a state of peace, harmony, and trust with nature.

Metalworks, such as protection amulets, offering bowls, butterlamps, and so forth, are often adorned with the eight auspicious emblems: the lotus, Dharma wheel, conch shell, precious vase, knot of infinity, two fishes, precious umbrella, and victory banner. These represent various auspicious spiritual qualities. The eight spokes of the wheel, for example, represent the eight facets of the eightfold path to enlightenment. The precious vase represents the ability to collect knowledge and spiritual realization. The conch shell represents the sound of truth; the manner in which the matrix of the conch begins at a point and swirls outward represents how all things begin in emptiness or ultimate reality and emanate outward into the conventional world. Its white color represents the natural purity of all phenomena and how the Dharma teachings restore the mind to awareness of that natural purity.

Ritual implements, such as the vajra and bell (see page 115), also have their symbolism. In general, the vajra represents male energy, which is to be transformed into compassion, and the bell represents female energy, to be transformed into wisdom. Holding the vajra in the right hand and bell in the left symbolizes bringing the male and female energies of the body into balance, and spiritually integrating the forces of compassion and wisdom. Both the vajra and bell have five spokes: one in each of the directions, as well as one down the center. This represents how the path to enlightenment takes the five negative mental states—ignorance, attachment, aversion, pride, and jealousy—and transforms these into the five wisdoms—wisdom of the sphere of truth, wisdom of distinguishing awareness, wisdom of equality, wisdom of the mirror-like nature of things, and wisdom that accomplishes all actions. Most tantric implements carry a symbolism that reflects these five wisdoms.

In this way the implications of the spiritual process are drawn into and reflected from within every piece of Tibetan sacred art.

❧

CHAPTER FIVE

CREATING SACRED IMAGES

Photo credit © TIB

Altar

ATTITUDES AND THE WORKING ENVIRONMENT

In Tibet the work of creating a piece of Buddhist art was considered a sacred undertaking and an act of great merit for both the artist and the patron of the piece.

A patron could commission a painting or statue for any of a number of reasons. Perhaps the most common was to decorate the household shrine room. Most Tibetan houses set aside a space for this purpose. At the very least, every Tibetan home, even the tents of the nomads, had an altar, and this would have at least three objects on it: a stupa, a scripture, and a Buddha statue, respectively representing the mind, speech, and form of the enlightened beings. The Buddha image would be placed in the center of the altar, with the stupa to its left (the viewer's right), and the scripture to the Buddha's right. In prosperous households the stupa and statue would be made of bronze, silver, or even gold; in more modest households they would be made of clay or wood. Most household temple rooms would also have a number of tangka paintings hanging above the altar.

Sacred art objects were often commissioned to honor the birth of a child, and as an act of merit to ensure the child's health and success.

Similarly, a piece could be commissioned as an act of merit on behalf of a recently deceased relative or friend. Sometimes a piece would be offered as a gift to a teacher, student, friend, or relative, or as a marriage gift, with the thought that a strong spiritual link would thus be established between the giver and the receiver. The Dalai Lama, for example, has many tangka paintings and bronze statues made each year, which he gives as presents to disciples and to Tibet supporters around the world; naturally, those who receive such a gift from him regard it as a symbol of a special spiritual bond. Most high lamas do the same.

The motivation of the artist who creates a piece of sacred art is considered to be very important. At the very least, he or she should have an attitude of devotion during the execution of the work, and should recite the mantras associated with the divinity form being created. Many artists even undertake a short meditation retreat before beginning a work, especially if the piece to be created is of a tantric nature.

Tibetans have a very specific policy toward the monetary exchange that takes place between the artist and client. Sacred art pieces should not be made and then placed for sale on the open market. Instead, a client or patron should first commission a piece, the price for the effort and materials should be clearly established in advance, and only then should the work be done. Great artists obviously can command a higher price for their work than can a lesser artist; but there should be no excessive demonstrations of greed or arrogance on the part of either parties involved. Both should

regard their relationship as being of a spiritual nature and proceed on the basis of the motivation to strengthen goodness and enlightenment in the world. A mediocre work from an artist of a pure heart is held in higher regard than a better one from an artist considered to be greedy and nonspiritual.

This attitude has continued in the refugee communities of India and Nepal. Artists who make pieces for open distribution are regarded as corrupt by the community, and those who honor the traditional approach are held in high regard. In fact, very few Tibetans deviate from the tradition. The hundreds of paintings to be found in the tourist shops of Delhi and Kathmandu today are usually made by young Indians and Nepalis in what only can be described as sweatshops; it is very rare to discover a piece of quality among them. Some Tibetan antique dealers do operate on the scene, but they are looked down upon and sometimes are even ostracized by their own people.

The traditional artists generally are rewarded for their integrity by receiving the patronage of the community, and receive so many commissions that they are booked for several years in advance.

THE LEARNING PROCESS

The legend of the creation of the first painting of the Buddha, known in Tibetan as *Chu-len-ma*, or "Taken from Water," states that it was painted from a reflection of the Buddha in a pool of water. The traditional account states

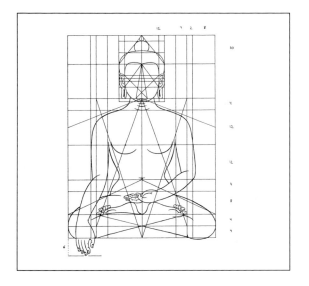

that the artists who prepared that first image began by creating a grid pattern of the Buddha's precise shape by means of wading into the pool and taking finger-width measurements of the reflection, and that the grid thus formulated has acted as a guide for all future generations.

Although some Tibetan artists were monks, the majority were lay people, with the tradition

being passed within the family from generation to generation. Outside apprenticeships were accepted, but this was never done lightly and was akin to a lifetime commitment on the part of both student and teacher.

Most master artists kept a studio within their home, where they would work together with their students and apprentices. Large commissions for temple or monastery work would usually entail that the master and his many students take up temporary residence on the precincts of the site until the project was com-

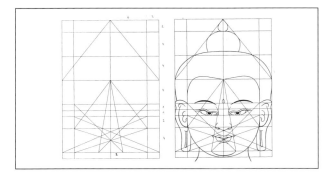

pleted. The senior students and young apprentices would do most of the work, with the master supervising and adding final touches.

The first year of an art student's training would be dedicated to helping the master and senior students around the studio in whatever way possible. This entailed mostly menial tasks such as grinding the materials to be used in preparing color pigments, helping to prepare canvases, and in general getting a feel for the artistic process. After that he or she would be introduced to drawing techniques.

Great emphasis was placed on the period of learning to draw correctly. The training would begin with mastering the classical buddha face, which usually required about three months, and then went on to the unclothed buddha form, to which a further three months was dedicated. Next came a study of the robes and the subtle flow of their lines. After this he or she would be introduced to other buddha forms, such as Amitabha, that have similar bodily proportions and appearance but different hand postures. Then would come the simple bodhisattva figures, such as Avalokiteshvata, Manjushri, Arya Tara, and so forth. This would be followed by the more complex divinities, including the wrathful figures and the meditational deities, many of which have numerous faces and arms.

This rigid and strict training in first establishing a strong basis in drawing was common to students of both painting and sculpture. After completing it, the apprentice painter would progress to working with color; the apprentice sculpture would then progress to working with clay, wax, wood, and metals.

Types of Sacred Tibetan Paintings

Sacred paintings generally appeared in three different media: as frescoes on temple walls; as tangka paintings; and as illustrations to scriptures. There is also a tradition of making temporary mandala sand paintings on a flat surface from colored sands; this rare art is discussed in the next chapter.

The Tibetan word *tangka* is a term that refers to a work done on cloth and set in a silk or cotton frame. Western art historians refer to tangkas as "Tibetan painted scrolls," because they are rolled up like scrolls when not in use. In fact, there were several different types of tangkas, only one of which was painted. The most expensive tangkas in Tibet were known as *lhendrup tangka*, or applique tangkas (see page 157), which were created by means of cutting pieces of colored silks into the desired shapes and then sewing these together into the deity forms. The next most expensive tangka was known as *takdrup tangka*, and was made by a weaving process. After this came *tshemdrup tangka*, which was made by an embroidery technique. Then came the *tsondrup tangka*, which was painted on cloth canvas. Finally, there were *shingpar tangka*, or wood-block prints on cloth.

Our exhibit emphasizes painted tangkas. These are generally held in the highest regard by Western collectors, and their beauty is perhaps more accessible to the Western eye.

Painted tangkas again are of various types. The most common are known as *chu-tson tangka*, or water-color paintings, in which the paints used are generally made from vegetable and mineral extracts. A popular form for the depiction of wrathful deities is the *nagtang*, or "black tangkas," which gain their name from the fact that they are painted with gold-dust ink (and also sometimes vermillion) on a black background (see page 129). Then there is *tsel-tang*, which are prepared by painting in gold-dust ink on a red vermillion background (see page 113). We have not provided examples of all of these in our exhibit because our purpose is not anthropological or academic.

Tangkas could be prepared either as individual pieces or as sets. A private individual would usually commission a single tangka, or perhaps a small set. Sets were more commonly found in large monasteries and temples, which had the space to hang them. Some tangka sets were extremely large, such as the 108 tangkas in the set known as *Paksam Trishing*, or "The Wish-fulfilling Tree," which depicts the life of the Buddha in 108 episodes. A smaller set illustrating the life of the Buddha is known as the *Dzepa Chonyi*, or "Twelve Wondrous Deeds," which celebrates the twelve major events in the Buddha's life in a set of five, seven, or thirteen tangkas. Similar sets are used to present the biographies of later great Buddhist masters, as well as cycles of tantric deities, traditional groupings of bodhisattvas, and so forth.

We have included two sets in our exhibit: "Buddha and the Sixteen Arhats," known in Tibetan as *Neyten Chudruk*, which is here presented as a set of seven tangkas (see page 91); and a set of five tangkas representing the Five Visions of Tsongkhapa (see page 79), known in Tibetan as *Jey Zikpa Ngaden*, or "The Five Visions of the Precious Master."

MATERIALS AND PIGMENTS

To make a tangka painting, an artist requires a good canvas. Generally an artist would make his own canvases. He would begin with a piece of good-quality cotton or silk cloth, and stretch this in a wooden frame. He would then apply a thin mixture of glue and calcium chalk to the cloth in order to create a base strong enough to support the paints yet subtle enough to allow the finished piece to be rolled up for storage when the painting was not being displayed. Generally several canvases are prepared at once, and then used as required. These are kept in their wooden stretching frames until the paintings planned for them are complete. The painting work is done on them while they are in their wooden stretching frames.

Again, most artists prefer to prepare their own paints. Traditionally the colors are made from the powders of precious and semi-precious stones, although some are also made of vegetable extracts. Blue generally is made from azurite (Tib., *do-ting*), with various shades being achieved by varying the length and intensity of the grinding process. Yellow is made from orpiment yellow (Tib., *ba-la*), which is the natural trisulfate of arsenic. Green is produced from malachite (Tib., *do-drang*), and its various shades are effected by mixing this with either plant extracts or arsenic. Minium (Tib., *li-tri*), also known as red lead, is used in the preparation of orange colors, and usually is imported from Nepal. Vermillion (Tib., *tsel*) is the source of the pigments of most red colors used in tangka painting. Yellow ocher (Tib., *nang-pa*) is used as a background underpaint wherever large quantities of gold-dust paint are to be used. White is created from a variety of substances, including calcinated animal bone, white earth (Tib., *ka-rak*), and white marble powder. Black mostly is produced from ash and soot. Indigo imported from India is also popular, as are numerous other plant and animal extracts, such as saffron.

The Process of Creating a Tangka

The first step in creating a tangka painting involves making an outline of the planned composition on the canvas.

This begins with fixing particular geometrical lines on the canvas. This is done with the help of a string saturated with a colored chalk; the string is laid in place and then snapped against the canvas, thus leaving a light impression on it. First the diagonals are set in place, so as to ascertain the center point of the canvas, and then the vertical and horizontal lines are emplaced. This facilitates the synchronicity that is a basic character of a good Tibetan painting. After this, the grids used in creating the specific figures are penciled in, with the grid for the central figure being created first, followed by those for the smaller figures to be placed above and/or below. Finally, the basic outline for the background is penciled in.

When the artist is happy that the basic layout of the tangka is complete, he goes over the outline of the desired pattern with a light red ink and cleans away the earlier work lines that had been used. He thus is left with an exact line drawing of the planned piece.

The next stage of the work involves the application of the paints. This is done by first coloring in the larger background areas, such as the earth and sky, and then any flowers, trees, or animals used in the background. Depth is accomplished principally by means of shading. Eventually only the outlines of the sacred figures are left unpainted. He then begins working on each of these, again beginning from the out-

side and working in toward the center of each. Thus first he paints the halos, then the robes, then the exposed bodily parts, and so forth.

When all the basic work has been completed, he strengthens the main lines of the images on the tangka by applying a thin touch of gold

Tangka painter at work

to them. In fact, the pigment usually is bonded gold dust that has been burnished with powder from a semi-precious stone in order to heighten its luster. The robes receive a golden outline, and might even be given an embellishment of flower patterns or some other decora-

Photo credit © TIB

tion in order to make them sparkle. Bodily ornaments, such as the crown, necklace, bracelets, and so on worn by a bodhisattva or tantric deity, and any implements held, probably are painted in this gold ink.

Often much of the easier work is done by senior students and apprentices, with the master artist coming in only at the end of the process to do the faces, hands, and gold work. He does, of course, supervise the entire process, and correct any mistakes that he feels have been made.

The last thing to be painted in is the eyes. When these are finished the tangka is considered to be formally complete.

Often the artist writes three mantric syllables—om, *ah*, and *hum*—on the back of the canvas at the sites of the forehead, throat, and heart of any gurus, buddhas, or other divine figures, to symbolize the pure nature of enlightened body, speech, and mind. Sometimes a patron might request that this final detail be left for a lama to complete.

When the painting is finished it is removed from its wooden frame and sent to a tailor to receive a brocade frame. Probably in ancient times the cloth frame was made of a simple cotton, but during the reign of King Trisong Deutsen in the mid-eighth century China had to pay an annual tribute to Tibet of fifty-thousand rolls of silk brocade, and the Tibetans quickly developed a taste for good brocades.

Generally the frame consists of two narrow strips on the inside—one yellow and one red—and then a larger blue border on the outside. Sometimes a brocade patch is sewn into the blue section below the painting, to represent the "door" to the spiritual world being symbolized by the image. A thin veil made from yellow and red silk is hung over the tangka to protect it from damage when it is not being viewed; this would be gathered up and tucked in at the top of the tangka when the piece was hung on display. In addition, two ribbons are hung down the front of the tangka to symbolize the process of bringing the blessings of the spiritual world into our mundane dimension. A supporting bar made of wood is sewn into the top of the brocade frame so that the painting will hang without drooping or creasing, and another is sewn into the bottom of the frame to act as a weight. Usually the ends of the lower wooden bar are longer than the cloth frame, so that approximately an inch of wood sticks out on each side of the tangka; either a silver or brass knob is fitted to each end as an adornment, and also as added weight.

THE STATUE-MAKERS

The Tibetan word for a painter is *lha tripa*, which translates as "divinity scribe." The word for a sculptor is *lha dzowa*, which translates as "deity-maker."

Statues of the buddhas, bodhisattvas, great lamas, and saints, as well as of the various types of meditational deities and Dharma Protectors, were made from a range of materials. The most popular media were clay, bronze, copper, silver, and gold. For some reason the

Tibetans didn't work very much with either wood or stone. Wood was reserved largely for carved columns in temples, as well as for carved bookcovers (see page 143), woodblocks for printing, and so forth; and stone was reserved largely for use as building materials. The reason probably is rooted in history. Tibet acquired its statue-making skills primarily from Nepal, and not from India or China; metal is the substance of choice in Nepal, whereas stone and wood are more popular in India and China. Tibet mainly followed the Nepalese tradition.

Every Tibetan monastery had a number of large clay statues. Clay was a popular material, for it was inexpensive, easily worked, and quite durable at Tibet's high, dry altitude. The clay itself was in fact a combination of earth, paper fiber, and a glue binder. Clay statues would have to be prepared on the site where they were to be housed, for once completed they could not be moved long distances because of their fragility. However, when safely placed in its permanent seat, a clay statue could last for centuries without degeneration.

The finished clay image would not be heated or baked, but simply allowed to dry. It would then be given a cover of paint, bestowing upon it a well-finished and sophisticated presence. Clay statues of lamas or buddhas would generally be displayed in a set of monkrobes; statues of bodhisattvas and tantric deities would be decorated in silk brocades. Sometimes a small bronze statue, as well as other consecrated substances, would be built inside the clay image as a blessing.

An unusual use for large clay images was housing mummies. For example, all ninety-seven patriarchs of the Gelukpa School, or "Ganden Throne Holders," were mummified after death.

The mummification process begins with passing mercury through the corpse by pouring it into the mouth. This cleans and disinfects both the stomach and the intestines. Then the body is dried in salt. During this process it is placed in the meditation posture, with legs crossed and so forth. When it has been properly dried in this way, a clay statue is built up around it. This is then gilded, dressed in monk-robes and the yellow pandit hat, and placed in the special chapel reserved for it. One cannot discern from looking at the image that it contains a mummified corpse; it looks the same as any other clay statue of a lineage master.

Another interesting tradition is that of *tsa-tsa* statues. These are pressed from clay by means of a mold. Religious practitioners do this as an act of devotion, pressing some thousands, for example, as a preliminary to meditation retreat. Also, sometimes it is recommended that the ashes of a cremated relative be mixed with clay, pressed into *tsa-tsa* statues, and the statues placed in holy places. Similarly, the ashes of a cremated lama were sometimes mixed with clay and pressed into *tsa-tsa* statues; some of these would be placed in a special reliquary at a holy site, and the remainder given to disciples, who would have them painted and then kept them on their altar.

Metal, however, was the preferred material of Tibetan sculptors. Smaller images were made by means of the lost wax technique, and larger images by means of hammering and shaping. We have examples of both of these in our exhibit. Whereas clay statues usually were solid, metal statues generally were hollow inside, with the base of the image being left open so that various sacred substances could later be placed inside of it.

An alloy made by combining brass, copper, and zinc was the most commonly used metal. Different tones were achieved by varying the amount of the ingredients and controlling the temperature at which the fusion was effected. Often as many as a dozen other metals were added to the formula in small quantities for various effects. Southern Tibet had a tendency to work more with copper than did other parts of the country, and Eastern Tibet had a tendency to use more brass.

Tsa tsa mold of the First Dalai Lama

Photo credit © TIB

After a cast statue came out of its mold it was finished with a hammer and chisel in order to provide it with a heightened precision in detail. Usually the face was given a coat of gold paint, with the eyes and mouth colored in at the end in order to bring the image alive. Similarly, the faces of statues made from hammered alloy were also given gold finishes.

Statues made of pure silver and gold were also known, although obviously their prohibitive cost meant that they were not as common. However, most large temples had at least one image made of pure gold, and some of these were quite large.

For example, when the First Dalai built Tashi Lhunpo in 1447, he made a life-size Tara statue out of pure gold. Similarly, when the Second Dalai Lama built Chokhor Gyal Monastery below the Oracle Lake, he announced that he wanted to have a Maitreya statue made out of pure gold for it. One of his wealthy patrons offered to sponsor the work, but the Second Dalai Lama refused, saying that he would prefer for each of his disciples and devotees across the country to donate a small piece of their personal jewelry for the purpose, in order for them to be able to make a karmic connection with Maitreya Buddha. The process of collection began, and within a year several thousand *sho* of gold were forthcoming, a quantity almost equivalent to a ton.

Although small metal statues would usually be made from a single cast, larger images would be created in pieces and then assembled.

THE CALLIGRAPHIC ARTS AND WOODBLOCK PRINTS

Our exhibit also includes two Tibetan texts that illustrate the important art of calligraphy, as well as one that is a woodblock print.

Calligraphy was ranked with the highest of arts. An apprentice calligrapher, just like an apprentice painter or statue-maker, would be expected to undertake a long and exacting training.

The Tibetan script is phonetic, and is based upon Gupta Sanskrit from India; it is not pictorial, like Chinese or Japanese. In fact, the Chinese script was banned from Tibet in 792; thereafter it was used only in letters of communication with the Chinese court, and even then only when these were sent in Chinese translation. Tibetan, like English, is read from the top left of the page to the top right.

Most texts prepared by a calligraphic process are also adorned with exquisite miniature paintings on the first pages, as well as on the closing page. The inks used are often made of silver or gold dust, or the powders of precious or semi-precious gems (see page 143). The paper is usually hand-made from wood pulp, although rice paper was not unknown. The calligrapher would usually write on only one side of a sheet, and then two sheets would be glued together back-to-back in order to form a page.

Copying sacred scriptures is considered to be a form of meditation and an act of great merit. This is the case not only within Tibetan Buddhism, but also within the traditions of China, Japan, Vietnam, and so forth.

Prior to Lama Tsongkhapa, who founded the Gelukpa school in the early fifteenth century, all Tibetan scriptures were copied by hand. Calligraphy became less common after that, but not less prestigious. It has continued into the present generation, and a text prepared by a master calligrapher today is still regarded as a great and sacred art treasure.

The preparation of woodblocks for printing scriptures was painstaking and lengthy. First the text would be written by hand on thin paper, and this would be glued face-down on the wood. The paper would be thinned until the script showed through (in reverse), and then a wood-carver would complete the task. Some monasteries, such as Nartang and Dergey, had printing houses with the woodblocks of hundreds and sometimes even thousands of books, many of which were hundreds of pages in length. Books would never be bound; instead, they would be wrapped in a cotton or silk cloth when not in use. The blocks would last for centuries, and books could be printed from them to order.

Wrapped book

CHAPTER SIX

THE ART OF PAINTING WITH COLORED SANDS

Creation of a sand mandala

AN
EPHEMERAL
AND
UNIVERSAL
ART

Most venues hosting the Mystical Arts of Tibet exhibit are also hosting the lamas to create an on-site mandala sand painting. On previous world tours they have constructed several dozen such sand paintings. Settings have been as diverse as the Field Museum of Natural History, Chicago; the Tampa Museum of Art, Florida; the CNN Building, Atlanta; the Museum of Fine Arts, Salt Lake City; the Indianapolis Art Museum, Indiana; the Gordon Snellgrove Gallery, Saskatoon, Canada; the Unitarian Universalist Church, Jacksonville, Florida; and the Miami Dade Community College, Miami. Sand mandalas have also been made in shopping malls, university campus foyers, prisons, and similarly "unartistic" places. The idea in tantric Buddhism is that all the world is equally sacred, and that any place benefits from a mandala sand painting.

In his commentary to the empowerment ceremony of the *Guhyasamaja Tantra* the Seventh Dalai Lama noted:

> The empowerment ceremony may be performed

On the basis of a drawn or painted mandala,
A mandala made of colored powders or
sands,
Or a mandala created through visualization.

In other words, a mandala may be created in any of these various media. The most visually striking is that made from colored sands, in which millions of grains are painstakingly placed on a flat surface by means of a funnel pen.

A traditional and prescribed iconography is followed that includes geometric shapes such as squares, circles, and a multitude of ancient spiritual symbols, all of which represent the inherent harmony of being and the enlightenment path.

The process of creating a sand mandala takes four monks approximately a week to complete. Then, as soon as it is finished and its purpose served, it is almost immediately swept up and poured into a river in order to symbolize the impermanence of all that exists. The waters carry the empowering energies throughout the world as a blessing for peace, healing, and harmony.

Sand painting is an ancient art, for we see it throughout the Himalayan and Central Asian regions in primitive forms that point to a pre-historic cultural root. The Native North Americans, for example, carried an early form of it with them when they migrated across the Bering Strait 15,000-20,000 years ago. It is common throughout India, and is used in a large variety of ceremonies, including those in celebration of birth, marriage, death, and so forth. The Tibetans do not use it in these secu-

lar ways; for them it is always associated with a particular tantric application involving transformation, healing, and enlightenment.

Purposes and Types of Mandala Sand Paintings

In Tibet, mandala sand paintings would be created for a number of purposes. For example, one could be made for use in a tantric empowerment ceremony, or for a blessing during a group meditation retreat. A mandala of the Healing Buddha could be made for empowerment and consecration of medicines, or as a preliminary to a ritual healing ceremony. A local community might commission one as part of a ceremonial ritual for world peace, prosperity, or the mitigation of natural calamities. In brief, there are as many purposes as there are needs in the human community.

The Sanskrit term for a sand painting is *mandala*, which means cosmogram or sacred circle. There are many types of mandalas. As we saw earlier in Chapter Two, the Mantrayana speaks of four classes or divisions of the tantras, and each class has a large number of tantric systems. Each individual system represents or emphasizes the cultivation and expression of a particular enlightenment quality. For example, Avalokiteshvara represents compassion, Manjushri is wisdom, Vajrapani is strength, Amitayus is longevity, the Medicine Buddha is healing, and so forth. Each of these systems has its own mandala.

In general, all mandalas have outer, inner,

and secret meanings. On the outer level they represent the world in its divine form; on the inner level they represent a map by which the ordinary human mind is transformed into the enlightenment experience; and on the secret level they depict the primordially perfect balance of the subtle energies of the body and the clear light dimension of the mind. The creation of a sand painting is said to effect a purification and healing on these three levels.

Each mandala can be prepared in one of four ways to symbolize one of the *trinley*, or enlightened activities: pacification, increase, power, and wrath. In other words, the mandala of Avalokiteshvara, which represents compassion, can do so as (1) compassion as a force to bring peace, (2) compassion as a force to increase good qualities, (3) compassion as an authoritative principle, and (4) compassion as forcefulness. A metaphor given in the scriptures is the four ways by which a mother deals with a difficult child. In all four modes her basic motivation is love and compassion, but in the first mode of expression she uses this force to quiet the child. In the second mode she uses her love to divert it to other creative endeavors, in the third mode she behaves authoritatively, and in the fourth she gives the child a spanking. All four are expressions of the same motivation of love and compassion. Which of the four *trinley* is being emphasized is expressed in the mandala sand painting by changing the base color used: white for pacification, yellow for increase, red for power, and dark blue for wrath.

SUBSTANCES USED

The Tibetan name for mandala sand painting is *dul-tsun-kyil-khor*, which translates as "mandala from colored powders." These powders can be made from any of a number of materials. In ancient India, kings would have their mandalas made from ground jewels or semi-precious stones. Thus lapis lazuli would be used for the blues, rubies for the reds, and so forth.

The most popular substance with the Tibetans is white marble that has been ground and then dyed. In India this is easily and cheaply acquired from the refuse produced by marble quarries. Otherwise, a fine, pure-white beach sand is a good alternative. The quality of whiteness is important, as otherwise the sand does not take to the dying process satisfactorily.

Other popular substances include powdered flowers, herbs, or grains and various powdered and colored stones.

THE PROCESS

Usually the mandala sand painting is created on a flat wooden platform that is about two or three feet high and four or five feet square on the top. The monks begin by laying down the basic construction lines, almost like an architect would prepare a blueprint of a building under construction. A line drawing of the entire mandala is then created with a white chalk pencil.

After this, the process of laying in the sand begins. This is accomplished by pouring the

Photo credit © TIB

Four monks working on a sand painting

sand through a metal funnel, known as a *chang-bu*. The funnel has one thick end, in which the sand is placed, and one thin end, from which it is poured. The top shaft has rivets along its surface, and the artist drags a thin metal tool across this in order to create a vibration. This causes the sand to roll out of the thin end of the funnel in a fine line, almost like ink flowing from a pen.

The artists begin the work from the inside of the design and work outward, to symbolize how at birth a child is just a drop of sperm and ovum and then steadily grows, until eventually the entire universe becomes experienced through the senses. When eventually the mandala has been completed, its purpose served, and the time for dismantling it has arrived, the sands are swept up from the outside toward the center, to symbolize how in old age and at the time of death everything once

more returns to the primordial source at the center of the heart.

Usually various rituals are performed at both the beginning and the conclusion of the work. The preliminaries include ritual music, and sometimes also sacred dance, in order to claim the site for the work, ask the local spirits for their permission and blessings, and invoke the forces of goodness and enlightenment as witnesses to the meritorious undertaking. Prior to dismantling the mandala another ceremony is performed in order to give thanks to the local spirits for their cooperation and to dedicate any meritorious energy that has been generated to the fulfillment of universal benefit, healing, and peace. The sands are swept up and carried in a vase to a nearby body of water, where they are deposited.

In addition to symbolizing the impermanence of things, the dismantling of the mandala symbolizes the ultimate empty nature of phenomena: how all things come out of nothingness and eventually return to it.

Patrons of, participants in, and witnesses to the creation and destruction of a mandala sand painting are purified and uplifted by the powers of the sacred energies involved. The area in which the art is performed is similarly transformed. Local spirits and deities are delighted, and send their blessings for peace and prosperity. The buddhas and bodhisattvas look down from their pure lands and release a shower of enlightenment energies. In brief, many benefits of both a temporal and spiritual nature are produced and the forces of goodness and light are strengthened.

CHAPTER SEVEN

SACRED MUSIC SACRED DANCE FOR WORLD HEALING

Lama temple musicians

SINGING IN CHORDS

The world tours of the Drepung Loseling monks began as a sharing of their ancient traditions of sacred music and dance for world healing and peace. As Geshe Lobsang points out in his preface, the elders of the monastery felt that this would be an appropriate way for the monastery to make a contribution to the international situation in the present troubled times. Most cities that host the exhibit will also host a performance of sacred music and dance, so it is appropriate to say something on this tradition here.

Drepung Loseling Monastery was the largest monastic institution in recorded history, with a population that generally stood at somewhere between nine and twelve thousand monks. It was the biggest of the three monastic universities of the Lhasa area: Ganden (founded 1409), Drepung (founded 1416), and Sera (founded 1419). Each of these three had two major wings, making six *dra-tsangs*, or colleges. The six had the distinction of being higher training grounds for the best monk students of not only Tibet, but of all Central Asia, from Siberia to Himalayan India. Every monk in the ten thousand monasteries of this vast area had a *kong*, or hereditary right, to admission to one of these six colleges. Drepung Loseling was the largest of the six, and in fact was as big as the other five combined.

Ganden, Drepung, and Sera, combined with their two associated tantric colleges, Gyuto and Gyumey, have many distinguishing characteristics. Musically they were unique in that all five preserved the tradition of multiphonic chanting known in Western musicology circles as "overtone singing" in which each singer intones a base note that is two octaves below middle C, while shaping the vocal cavity in such a way as to amplify two of the natural overtones that are produced, thus in effect singing in a complete chord. The Tibetans are the only people known to possess this extraordinary ability.

Drepung had the honor of leading the Monlam Chenmo, or Great Prayer Festival, Tibet's largest annual sacred celebration. The festival was created by Lama Tsongkhapa and first held in Lhasa in 1410, but quickly became emulated by all spiritual communities throughout Central Asia. From the time of the Second

Dalai Lama in the early sixteenth century it was led by Drepung Loseling, which has given the monks of Loseling a unique position among Tibet's multiphonic singers.

THREE DIMENSIONS OF DREPUNG LOSELING

The main assembly hall at Drepung Loseling hosted only vocal music. Musical instruments were not used; the multiphonic singing was all that was allowed. Anywhere from five to ten thousand monks could be heard singing with this unique technique at major gatherings.

In addition, Loseling had twenty-three *kham-tsens*, or departments, each of which represented a specific area of Central Asia. This administrative structure ensured that the monks who joined the twenty-year training program at Loseling would not lose their local dialects, and that when they eventually returned to their homelands as teachers they would not sound like foreigners. Each of these departments had its own temple; these temples were the forums in which vocal music was combined with the instrumentation for which Tibet has become known around the world: twelve-foot longhorns, (*dung-chen*), a type of high-tone horn (*gya-ling*); a large variety of cymbals (*boob*) and drums (*nga*); various bells (*dilbu*); and so forth. These *kham-tsen* maintained the rituals, prayers, and ceremonies associated with its home region. Moreover, each *kham-tsen* contained a number of *la-brang*, or residences of the incarnate lamas; each of these in turn had its own chapel, where the rituals associated with its incarnate lama were held. This again combined multiphonic vocalization with instrumentation.

Finally, each of the three great monastic universities had a large number of affiliate monasteries scattered throughout Central Asia, from which its young monks were drawn and to which its

Drepung Loseling Monastery, Lhasa

elderly teachers were sent after completion of their studies. The larger of these were represented by an incarnate lama who had a base in and received his higher training from one of the three and was founded by the first incarnation in that lama's rebirth lineage.

Loseling had more than two thousand affiliates of this nature. Many of these were small, with only a dozen or so monks. Others were quite large, with a thousand or more inhabitants. Most had populations somewhere between these numbers, with anywhere from twenty to a hundred monks. It was in these affiliate monasteries that the annual sacred dances were held, and not in Drepung Loseling itself.

The world tours of sacred music and dance undertaken by the monks of Drepung Loseling combine these three elements: the multiphonic singing as practiced in Loseling's main assembly hall; the vocalization and instrumentation held in the temples of the departments;

and the annual sacred dances held in the regional affiliate monasteries.

PERFORMING SACRED MUSIC AND SACRED DANCE

Ancient societies throughout the world have held that the performance of sacred music and dance is a source of great merit for human society, bringing the energies of the divine realms into the world of humans. Ceremonial performances of this nature can be seen in the societies of our North American indigenous peoples, as well as in the ancient shamanic societies of Africa, Australia, Central and South America, and Asia. The larger performances are usually done in accordance with solar and lunar cycles. However, they can also be performed on any occasion of special need.

In Tibet, most sacred performances were done

on an annual basis, and usually in conjunction with the lunar calendar. An example is the Monlam Chenmo, or Great Prayer Festival of Lhasa, which began with the new moon of every new year and continued for three weeks. Almost all of Central Asia's smaller monasteries had similar religious festivals. Some involved only music; others included sacred dance. These arts were thought to contribute to the peace and harmony of the area, as well as to purification in the face of obstacles and hindrances, the prevention of natural disasters, and the strengthening of the forces of goodness and stability in the world.

THE MULTIPHONIC SINGERS

Tibetans give two different accounts of the origins of the multiphonic singing tradition. According to the first of these, the technique was developed by the ninth century Indian tantric master Krishnacharya, from whom one of the three lineages of Heruka Chakrasamvara is descended.

The second account states that it was developed in Tibet and arose from the visionary experiences of Lama Tsongkhapa during his five-year meditation in the Olkha mountains. According to this version, Tsongkhapa experienced a vision of the dakas and dakinis, and heard the multiphonic singing in his meditations. He learned to emulate the style, and then taught it to his chief disciples. It was transmitted over the centuries since that time to the present generation.

Evidence points to the second account as the more probable of the two. Multiphonic

singing seems to have existed in Tibet only in the four principal monasteries established by Tsongkhapa and his immediate disciples—Ganden, Drepung, Sera, and Gyumey—together with Gyuto, the tantric college that is an offspring of Gyumey.

Performing or hearing multiphonic singing is considered to be a transformative experience. The vibration that the music creates clears and balances the subtle body and brings the blessings of the dakas and dakinis from etheric dimensions into the human world. Negative energies are dispersed, and innate radiance and clarity are reinforced.

The training of young monks in multiphonic singing is dispensed rather informally. Essentially a youth who seems to show interest and vocal talents is taken under the wing of one of the elder master vocalists, and informally coached. If he progresses well, the various styles and vocal pieces are gradually taught to him, which he masters by memory. Tibet did have a form of musical notation, but learning it was not a prerequisite for the student with a strong memory.

The monk who ascends to the position of chief vocal master in Drepung Loseling is given a place of honor and power second only to that of the abbot. He is not chosen solely for vocal abilities; rather, when a chief vocal master retires, his successor is selected first by drawing up a list of all the master vocalists who are musically qualified for the position and then submitting the names on the list to paranormal testing, such as divinations performed by high lamas of the school. In recent years the Dalai

Lama himself has performed divinations for this purpose. The State Oracle may also be consulted. The outcome of the divinations will determine who gets the position.

INSTRUMENTATION

Again, the training of young monks in the art of playing sacred instrumental music is somewhat informal, with keen interest and a modicum of talent being the prerequisites. Instrumental music was played only in the temples of the individual *kham-tsens*, or departments, of Drepung Loseling, or in the chapels of the reincarnate lamas; it was rarely played in the main assembly hall, and thus is not an official part of the monastery's curriculum. An exception is the *Khadro Tenshug Garcham*, or Dance of the Rainbow Space Travelers, a longevity and healing dance performed in times of the illness of a senior lama or a serious astrological hindrance to his life. This dance, which involves five monks dressed in rainbow costumes, is supported musically by an orchestra playing drums and cymbals; it does not include the various horns and trumpets commonly used in the music played in the departmental temples and chapels. Another exception is when the *Lama Chopa*, or Guru Homage Feast, is done; this ritual is not an official activity of the monastery and is performed in Loseling only on rare occasions and in times of special need.

Thus, within the precincts of Drepung Loseling Monastery, instrumental music is performed mainly in the departments and incarnate lama chapels. The principal ritual in which it is used is the monthly invocation of the individual department's main guardian deities. A ritual of this nature usually requires an entire day. In addition, the monastery as a whole, the monks of a specific department, a lama residence, or even individual monks can always be commissioned to perform particular rituals for peace, healing, prosperity, and so forth, and usually rituals of this nature involve rich instrumentation.

SACRED DANCE

Finally, with the exception of the Dance of the Rainbow Space Travelers as mentioned above, sacred dance was not performed on Loseling grounds, but rather was the jurisdiction of the smaller provincial affiliates. Many of the affiliates held sacred dance festivals once or more annually. These could last anywhere from a day to a week, and went from predawn until after sunset.

Early Western writers referred to these monastic events as "devil dances," because they usually center around the Dharma Protector Spirit, or dharmapala, that is linked either to the monastery or to the region (see pages 111). As we saw in an earlier chapter, the Dharmapalas are sometimes emanations of the buddhas and sometimes worldly spirits who have been sworn to the protection of the spiritual tradition. Generally they are very wrathful in appearance, in order to signify their ability to eliminate negative forces, obstacles to well-being, illness, and so forth. Their essential nature is described as compassion manifest in a wrathful guise. Some of the Dharma Protectors, such as Mahakala, are said to be wrathful emanations of Avalokiteshvara, the Bodhisattva of Compassion. These Dharma Protector dances are not inventions of the Tibetans, as some Western anthropologists have suggested, but very much are based in the Indian tantric tradition. We see similar dances today in traditions such as the Shri Devi festivals of South India. Tibetans merely adapted them to their own environment and aesthetic sensitivity, and extended the tradition to incorporate some of their own Protective Spirits.

A number of the dances are historical in nature, and reenact pivotal spiritual events in Tibet's Buddhist unfolding. However, the performance of them is not done merely to celebrate or glorify those historical events, but rather to invoke the energies that inspired those moments of national transformation and to call them into the present era.

Perhaps the most widespread and popular sacred dance with all schools of Tibetan Buddhism is the Black Hat Dance, an exorcism of negative forces. Probably borrowed from Tibet's pre-Buddhist tradition of Bon, it was quickly redefined and given a Buddhist context. Tibetan texts mention it as being performed in annual festivals as early as the ninth century.

Dance of the Cemetery Lords

Many monasteries perform this dance annually on the last day of the year in order to eliminate any negative energy residual from the outgoing year. It can be performed by two, four, eight, sixteen, thirty-two, or sixty-four dancers. Each dancer carries a mystical dagger with which to pierce the ego, the force that carries old negativities into the present moment, and also carries a skull cup filled with blissful wisdom, the ambrosia by which ego is transcended. Thus the ancient dance is given a purely Buddhist perspective.

Another very popular dance in all schools of Tibetan Buddhism is *Durdak Garcham*, or Dance of the Cemetery Lords. Here monks dance in skeleton costumes and perform a dance that expresses the laws of impermanence or change. The Cemetery Lords are Dharmapala, or "Protectors of Truth," and call the local spirits to support and protect truth and goodness in the world.

Tibetan sacred dances are always being rewritten. The theory is that their choreography and music are not born in a conventional manner, but are first beheld by a great lama or yogi in deep states of vision and meditative trance. He then teaches them to disciples. The enactment of them creates a link to the tantric forces embodied in the dance, as well as to the meditative vision of the master who envisioned them.

Tibet's sacred art and its use of mystical symbols extended beyond the borders of what has been discussed in the preceding chapters. Some of these alternate media are included in our exhibit, and some are not.

One such area, and we have included several examples in the exhibit, lies in the realm of Tibetan carpets. These are often rich in mystical symbols, such as the swastika, the vase of immortality, the phoenix, and so forth. The swastika is an ancient Himalayan logo for stability, balance and strength. Its antiquity is indicated by the fact that Native North Americans carried it with them when they migrated here 15,000-20,000 years ago; we can see it today in cave and rock paintings in New Mexico, as well as on the blanket designs of the Navajo.

Another area is horse blankets and saddles. We have included a saddle once used by the Fifth Dalai Lama; on the stirrups we find engravings of the knot of infinity, which essentially is an extension of the swastika.

Jewelry is a third area that often combines utilitarian use with sacred symbolism. Tibetans believe that wearing jewelry of this nature protects the bearer from harmful spirits, calls the forces of goodness to his or her side, purifies the body's aura, and performs numerous other such beneficial roles.

An exquisite Tibetan art that we have not officially included in the exhibit, but which will be created at some sites when time so permits, is the making of butter sculptures. This is an ephemeral art that was very popular in Tibet, and was commonly seen at festivals. The Monlam Chenmo, or Great Prayer Festival, for example, often used butter sculptures that were several meters in height and were adorned by images of various buddhas, bodhisattvas, dharmapalas, and so forth, all of which were shaped from colored butter.

It is not possible to convey the full range of a civilization's artistic efforts in a traveling exhibit. We hope, however, that we will at least have succeeded in giving viewers a glimpse into the magic and wonder that was Tibet and a sense of the splendor achieved by its artists.

SECTION ONE:
PERSONAL OBJECTS OF H.H. THE DALAI LAMA

Guru Padma Sambhava and His Eight Emanations

Size: 16″ by 24″

Date: Early 1900s

This tangka, painted in bright powder colors with a liberal quantity of pure gold, is in the New Mentri style. The names of the individual eight emanations were added at a later date with bronze paint. The rich brocade frame is more recent.

Padma Sambhava is popularly known throughout the Himalayas as Guru Rinpochey. He is the forefather of all schools of Tibetan Buddhism, for it was his work in Tibet, Nepal, and Bhutan in the mid-eighth century that really secured the fledgling Dharma in the Land of Snow Mountains and set it on a sound footing.

The name "Guru Padma Sambhava" translates as "The Lotus-Born Master," and reflects the story of his birth. King Indrabhuti of Oddiyana (the Swat Valley of modern-day northeastern Pakistan, near the border with Afghanistan) was walking in the park one day when he discovered an infant by the lakeside lying in a bed of lotus flowers. The king adopted the child and raised him as his son. The legend grew that the child was born from a lotus.

As a youth the prince became a monk and completed his classical Buddhist studies at the famous Nalanda Monastic University in Central India. However, he found the monastic lifestyle to be unsuited to his personal character and therefore disrobed. Later he traveled extensively and studied with many of the greatest masters of his day from Burma to Afghanistan. Eventually he achieved enlightenment and became one of India's foremost spiritual figures.

In the mid-seventh century King Trisong Deutsen wished to construct Tibet's first monastery, but his efforts met with many obstacles and hindrances because of the magical rituals being performed by Bonpo priests who opposed the project. The Indian master Shantirakshita suggested that the king invite Padma Sambhava from India in order to overcome the forces of obstruction. Padma Sambhava came to Lhasa, overpowered the Bonpo magic by means of his own occult powers, and supervised the completion of Samyey Monastery. He performed numerous tantric rituals in order to invoke the Bonpo gods and pledge them to the service of the Dharma, and also in order to consecrate various holy places of practice throughout the country. In addition, he set up a committee of twenty-five translators and personally oversaw the rendition of many Buddhist texts from Sanskrit into Tibetan.

His aspect as "The Lotus-Born Master" is depicted by the central image in the painting. We see him dressed in royal garb yet bearing various religious implements, to indicate that he is both a prince and a spiritual master. His hat was given to him by the dakinis, or angels, and its various folds symbolize accomplishment of the spiritual path. His right hand is in the gesture of teaching, and holds a vajra, to symbolize compassion and power. His left holds a skull cup filled with the liquids of blissful wisdom and a vase filled with the nectars of immortality.

We see him surrounded by his eight manifestations, which represent eight different aspects of his life: (1) as a young monk (top center) wearing the hat of a mahapandita, which refers to his completion of the monastic education; (2) as the elder monk Sakya Sengey, or "Buddha's Lion" (top right), which symbolizes his later contribution to the monastic tradition; (3) as the yogi Nyima Odser, or "the Sunlight Guru" (top left), in which he holds the sun and uses its rays as a tether, indicating that he is a yogi with control over the physical elements; (4) as Pema Gyalpo, or the "Lotus-born King" (middle right), representing his miraculous birth, and also his later role as the king of Zahor, following his marriage to Princess Mandarava; (5) as Loden Choksee, or "Kingly Wisdom Lord," depicting his role as a teacher of royal families; (6) as the Dharma Protector Sengey Dradok, or "The Lion's Roar" (bottom right), showing how he used forceful means and tantric rituals to subdue the enemies of truth; (7) as Dorjey Drolo," or "The Blazing Thunderbolt" (bottom left), in which he is depicted as a wild spirit riding on a tiger, to symbolize how he used unconventional and wild means to convey truth to trainees; and (8) as Buddha Vajradhara in union with a consort (bottom center), which depicts his secret aspect as a fully accomplished master of tantric Buddhism.

Khedrub Jey's Five Visions of Lama Tsongkhapa

The next five tangkas belong to a set known in Tibetan as *Jey Zigpa Ngaden*, or "Five Visions of the Master." Two popular names used by Tibetans for Tsongkhapa are Jey Rinpochey and Jey Lama, which respectively translate as "The Precious Master" and "The Master Lama."

According to the legend, after Tsongkhapa passed away in 1419 his disciple Khedrub Jey on five occasions met with him in mystical states. His five visionary meetings became favorite subjects of artists throughout Central Asia. Each of the five reveals a different aspect of Tsongkhapa's persona and life's work. The stories of all five visions are told in Khedrub Jey's *Sangwai Namtar*, or *Secret Biography*.

Khedrub Jey is most remembered for his charisma as a teacher, as well as for the many excellent commentaries that he wrote on the tantric lineages that Tsongkhapa gathered together and elucidated. He played an important role in the education of the First Dalai Lama, who was the youngest of Tsongkhapa's five chief disciples. The First Dalai Lama completed many of his tantric studies under Khedrub Jey.

Khedrub Jey appears in various tangkas in our exhibit as part of Jey Yab Sey Sum, or "The Trio of the Precious Master and (his two chief) Disciples" (see page 159). As chief of the trio, Tsongkhapa represents the first head of the Gelukpa; his elderly disciple Gyaltseb Jey was his immediate successor; and the younger Khedrub Jey was the next successor to Tsongkhapa's Throne.

The set of paintings of Khedrub Jey's five visions of Tsongkhapa in our exhibit are all by the same artist. They were painted in the late 1800s and belonged to the previous Dalai Lama, the Great Thirteenth.

Khedrub Jey's First Vision.

Khedrub Jey's Second Vision.

Khedrub Jey's Third Vision.

Khedrub Jey's Fourth Vision.

Khedrub Jey's Fifth Vision.

79

Khedrub Jey's First Vision

Size: 16″ by 24″
Date: Late 1800s

Khedrub Jey's *Secret Biography* (*Sangwai Namtar*) states, "Some time after the precious master passed away Khedrub Jey was on a teaching tour. In his room one night thoughts of the Master weighed heavily on his mind. He reflected on how the sentient beings were low in merit and thus lack the fortune to meet with authentic masters. Collected phenomena are impermanent, yet people see them as permanent; and although all things are empty of true existence, they grasp at them as real. Possessions have no essence, yet they strive only to gather them. Praise and fame are like echoes in a cave, yet mindless beings chase them as though they were final attainments. Moreover, the Precious Master had elucidated the full range and most subtle points of the Buddha's tantric teachings, yet people seemed unable to appreciate what he had done, and instead followed inferior teachers who just spread confusion and fantasy, and were as attuned to real practice as animals. In their eagerness for wealth and offerings, they deceived people and were little better than thieves and bandits. They praised themselves and derided others, and spread sectarian feelings wherever they went. Their ways were more like those of dogs and pigs than spiritual masters, yet they publicly presented themselves as great meditators and saints. He burst into tears.... Suddenly Jey Lama appeared to him."

In this vision Tsongkhapa appeared in the form of a monk. He was seated on the back of a white elephant, his body shining with a golden light like that of a buddha, and the melodious sound of bells filled the air. He told Khedrub Jey not to be disheartened, and that if he were to concentrate on his teaching activities all would be well in the end. He advised him to read the mystical songs of Milarepa, Tibet's greatest yogi and poet, for strength and inspiration.

The white elephant in the image symbolizes the stable power of effective meditation. It also represents Tsongkhapa's future role as the eleventh of the thousand universal teachers of this world age. His dress as a mahapandita indicates his mastery of all the Buddhist arts and sciences. He holds the stems of lotuses that bear a scripture and a sword of wisdom, indicating that he is an emanation of Manjushri, the Bodhisattva of Wisdom.

Our artist's rendition of the vision depicts Buddha Maitrya sitting in the clouds above Tsongkhapa's left shoulder, his two hands in the teaching mudra, to indicate the special relationship that Tsongkhapa had throughout his life with Maitreya, and how he continually received teachings directly from him. Maitreya's hair is adorned with a stupa, symbolic of the enlightened mind.

The mandala deity Heruka Chakrasamvara dances in the sky above Tsongkhapa's right, indicating the emphasis that Tsongkhapa had placed upon the yogas of that tantric system. The Dharma Protector and Wealth God Vaishravana sits on a snow lion below, to signify that those who practice well will always have their basic needs provided for them. The snow lion symbolizes the natural abundance of nature; when meditators get snowed in during the winter and are cut off from all supplies, the snow lionesses come to their caves and feed them their milk, which possesses every healing and nutritional property. Similarly, a naga spirit holds up an offering from the waters of the lake, symbolizing how those who meditate always receive their basic needs.

❀

Khedrub Jey's Second Vision

Size: 16″ by 24″
Date: Late 1800s

Khedrub Jey was meditating on some of the subtle points in the Buddha's teachings. In particular, questions arose in his mind concerning specific points in tantric practice. He thought, "If only Jey Lama were here I would be able to clear up all my doubts. But he is gone, and there is nobody upon whom I can rely."

He arranged a special altar, prepared a mandala offering, and sent out many prayers. Suddenly a youthful and vibrant Tsongkhapa appeared to him. His form was like that of a sixteen-year-old youth, he was dressed in the robes of a monk, and was seated on a jeweled throne upheld by a host of youthful gods and goddesses.

The Secret Biography states, "Lama Tsongkhapa then proceeded to answer all his questions, resolve all his doubts, give him many tantric initiations, and impart numerous special teachings to him."

In the painting we see a tree with its flowers in full bloom standing to Tsongkhapa's right (the viewer's left), to symbolize the blossoming of the Dharma. The mandala deity Guhyasamaja is at the top of the tree, for this tantric system, with its doctrines of the illusory body and clear light yogas, was regarded by Tsongkhapa as the pinnacle of Buddha's teachings. The Buddha in the form of a monk is in the sky above Tsongkhapa's left shoulder, to indicate Tsongkhapa's work in the rejuvenation of the monkhood and a return to the pure teachings of the Buddha, from which the Tibetans had strayed. Below Tsongkhapa stands Mahakala, who is the Bodhisattva of Compassion in his wrathful emanation as a Dharma Protector, and who had pledged to protect and uphold Tsongkhapa's lineages.

To his left and right are mounds of wrathful and peaceful offerings.

❁

Khedrub Jey's Third Vision

Size: 16″ by 24″
Date: Late 1800s

Khedrub Jey's *Secret Biography* states, "One day Khedrup Jey was reading some of the texts written by Jey Lama on the two stages of the path (exoteric and esoteric). He became overwhelmed by the power and depths of Jey Lama's words: how his teachings had covered the full range of Sutrayana and Vajrayana doctrines, together with the four tantra divisions; how he had shown how the complete teachings of the Buddha could be carried into a single individual's enlightenment training; how he had presented all the trainings of both Sutrayana and Vajrayana, from the initial practice of developing a relationship with a spiritual master up to the final technique of great union, in such a way that they could be integrated in order to bring quick enlightenment of Buddha Vajradharahood in a single lifetime."

He thought to himself, "There has been no master equal to him even among the gurus of India, the early Kadampa lamas, or the two Mahamudra lineages." He was overcome by a wave of emotion, and tears flowed from his eyes and fell onto his lap.

Suddenly Tsongkhapa appeared to him in a vision. He was in the form of the Bodhisattva Manjushri, and was riding on a snow lion. He said, "My spiritual son, there is no need to cry. Instead, you should impart the teachings that you have received. In this age the sentient beings are of various qualities. Most don't think much about impermanence and the lower realms. They mainly chase possessions, fame, and self-glory. Beings are rare who appreciate that there is no end to worldly works. But do not be disheartened. Train those who come to you, and the forces of goodness will prevail." He then gave Khedrub Jey many teachings and initiations.

In the vision Tsongkhapa appears as Manjushri, for although he lived his life as though he were an ordinary monk, in fact he was an incarnation of the Bodhisattva of Wisdom. Thus here he appears in his real form. His right hand holds the stem of a lotus that blossoms beside his right shoulder; a wisdom sword stands in it, for he symbolizes the realization that cuts to the heart of enlightenment and severs all wrong understanding. The book in the lotus beside his left shoulder is the *Prajnaparamita Sutra*, or *Perfection of Wisdom Discourse*, in which Buddha most explicitly elucidated the emptiness doctrine. He rides upon a snow lion, the white color of which represents the natural purity of ultimate reality; the pink on the lion's belly represents the bliss that arises in the meditator's mind when ultimate reality is understood. The snow lion dances playfully, indicating the liberation that follows from wisdom.

Above Tsongkhapa's right shoulder is the mandala deity Kalachakra, or "The Mysterious Wheel of Time," an important tantric system that Tsongkhapa rescued from oblivion and made into one of the most popular tantric systems with all Tibetan schools. (This tantra is associated with the mythical land of Shambhala, from which James Hilton drew his inspiration in formulating the Shangri-la of his novel *Lost Horizons*.) Above Tsongkhapa's left shoulder sits Avalokiteshvara, the Bodhisattva of Compassion, to indicate that wisdom must never be separated from love and compassion.

Below Tsongkhapa the Dharma Protector Mahakala dances on a corpse. This aspect of Mahakala has special links with Drepung Loseling, and was strongly practiced by the early Dalai Lamas. Peaceful and wrathful offerings of the five senses lay respectively to the right and left of Mahakala.

✤

Khedrub Jey's Fourth Vision

Size: 16" by 24"
Date: Late 1800s

Khedrub Jey's *Secret Biography* reads, "On another occasion Khedrub Jey was thinking of Jey Lama. 'I wonder where the Master Lama is now, and when I will meet with him again.' Tears flowed from his eyes, and every hair on his body quivered with emotion. . . . Suddenly Jey lama appeared to him. He was riding on a tiger blazing with fierce energy, and was in the garb of a yogi. His body was reddish in color, and his eyes were wild and fierce. His right hand held a wisdom sword toward the sky, and his left held a skull cup filled with nectar at his heart. His hair was long, and was tied in a knot on top of his head, and he was dressed in ornaments of human bone. The eighty-four mahasiddhas surrounded him, and looked on with delight. He said, 'My spiritual son, there is no need for you to feel that we are separated. I am never far from you, and you never far from me. I have not left you and gone elsewhere. Whenever you want to see me, just read the texts on the two stages of tantric practice that I have written, and you can know that I am present. In general, the sentient beings of today are of small merit, and their minds are made coarse by the delusions. Your role is to place some of them in the gateway leading to enlightenment. Do that, and we will meet again soon in the Land of the Dakinis." He then gave him many special teachings and initiations.

In this painting Tsongkhapa is seen as a mahasiddha. As we saw in Part One, the mahasiddhas are Indian masters who transmitted the tantric lineages to the early Tibetan translators. Most of them were not monks; even those who were monks generally did not wear the conventional robes. They often lived in the jungles with the wild animals, and acquired their food from wherever they could. They are depicted in Tibetan art as wild, wrathful-looking characters who expressed their enlightenment in unconventional ways. In Khedrub Jey's vision Tsongkhapa is surrounded by the eighty-four Indian mahasiddhas, which is a list of the Indian tantric yogis who were most popular with the Tibetans; however, this aspect of the vision is not depicted in the painting.

Tsongkhapa rides on a tiger, a symbol of the energy and fierce boldness of the enlightened mind and the tantric path. The tiger is fearless, indicating how Tsongkhapa was fearless in giving the highest and most esoteric teachings and in undertaking the most intimidating Dharma activity. His ornaments are of human bone, symbolizing how he had transcended all conventional mortality; his necklace is a Dharma Wheel, to indicate that he mastered all aspects of Buddhist teachings. He holds a sword of wisdom in his right hand, for he is an incarnation of Manjushri, the Bodhisattva of Wisdom; and he holds a skull cup filled with blissful wisdom in the left, indicating that he has drunk of the most subtle of tantric yogas. A meditation belt hangs over his shoulder, perhaps in reference to his five-year meditation retreat in the Olkha mountains, where he lived solely on juniper berries.

Above the tree to Tsongkhapa's left is the mandala deity Tara in her tantric aspect, her full breasts exposed to indicate the nutritious and delicious taste of the milk of tantric practice. The mandala deity Vajrayogini dances in the sky above Tsongkhapa's right shoulder, her exquisite vagina exposed to indicate the blissful nature of tantric experience. The katvanga staff over her shoulder reveals the stages in tantric training, and she drinks the blood of tantric delight from a human skull cup, to show how her yogas bring every element of human experience into the blissful taste of wisdom. Her right hand holds a curved knife, with which she severs the ugly head of ego.

Below Tsongkhapa we see Palden Lhamo, a female Dharma Protector who has been propitiated by all the Dalai Lama incarnations and who is the goddess of the Oracle Lake. She rides her mule on a sea of flames, to indicate how she burns away obstacles wherever she goes.

The mirror, cymbals, conch shell, fruit, and scarf beside Palden Lhamo represent the offerings of the five senses.

Khedrub Jey's Fifth Vision

Size: 16″ by 24″
Date: Late 1800s

Khedrub Jey's *Secret Biography* states that on a fifth occasion he was caught up in intense memories of his guru Lama Tsongkhapa, and felt a tremendous yearning to be with him. He arranged a special altar, held up a golden mandala, and offered this prayer, "Father of the buddhas of the past, present, and future, sole refuge to the protectorless sentient beings, incomparable manifestation of the Bodhisattva Manjushri, master who is a Buddha Vajradhara, I call to you." Tsongkhapa suddenly appeared to him in a vision, as though floating in on a carpet of clouds. He was dressed in the robes of a monk, and was radiant with light. Khedrub Jey asked him, "Oh my precious guru, where are you now, and when can I join you?" Tsongkhapa replied, "In general, I have sent emanations to the Pure Land of Dakinis, the Pure Land of Joy, and also many places on earth. Even at this very moment one of my emanations is on the sacred Five-Peaked Mountain in China, giving teachings to 1,800 tantric monks. During the morning session he teaches on emptiness, the middle view, and the General Mahayana; during the afternoon session he teaches on the two yogic stages of the Guhyasamaja, the Heruka Chakrasamvara and Vajrabhairava tantric systems. You yourself should continue to teach. Make prayers that we meet again, and before long it will come to pass." He then gave Khedrub Jey many teachings and initiations.

For the remainder of his life Khedrub Jey continued to have visions of Tsongkhapa in which he could communicate with him directly. However, these first five visions remain special, because in all later experiences Tsongkhapa appeared in one of these same five forms.

The artist has brought several personal elements into his depiction of this fifth vision. For example, although Tsongkhapa is shown in his usual form, with his hands in the gesture of teaching the Dharma, his fingers hold the stems of lotus flowers that bear the sword of wisdom and the *Prajnaparamita Sutra*. Here we also see a white Tara in the right lotus and a green Tara in the left. Probably this is because Tara is a female buddha who symbolizes the activity of the enlightened beings, with her white emanation (the color of water) representing the longevity yogas and her green emanation (the color of wind) representing success in all endeavors; her twofold presence here is as an auspicious sign contributing to longevity and the successful completion of many creative deeds. Similarly, the tree growing to Tsongkhapa's left bears peaches, a symbol of longevity and immortality.

Tsongkhapa's throne is upheld by eight lions, two in each of the four directions. These symbolize the eight states of fearlessness, and convey to Khedrub Jey that he must learn to be brave and fearless in his life and work. The lion throne is especially linked to teaching.

Buddha Shakyamuni sits in the sky above the peach tree, to symbolize transcendence of grief, and a long life dedicated to the accomplishment of buddhahood. The mandala deity Yamantaka (see page 110) dances on the clouds in the space above Tsongkhapa's right shoulder (the viewer's left); Yamantaka was one of Tsongkhapa's main tantric practices, and is considered to be the wrathful form of Manjushri, of whom Tsongkhapa is an emanation. Kalarupa and Consort, Dharmapalas who are emanations of Yamantaka, are in the bottom center of the composition, to indicate the elimination of outer, inner, and secret obstacles.

Wrathful tantric offerings of the five senses—eyeballs, ears, nose, tongue, skin, and blood—fill a skull cup to Kalarupa's left, to symbolize how the objects of the senses should be dedicated to the enlightenment path. The eight auspicious symbols stand in a lotus growing from a pool to Kalarupa's left, to show that when all is done well in this way then everything becomes auspicious.

Buddha Shakyamuni and the Sixteen Arhats

The following seven paintings belong to a set known in Tibetan as *Neyten Chudruk*, or "The Sixteen Arhats." These sixteen have been a favorite subject of artists in India, China, Tibet, Mongolia, and Nepal for well over a thousand years.

As we saw earlier in Chapters Two and Four of Part One, the arhats are the saints of early Buddhism who accomplished the state of nirvana, and embody the qualities of gentleness and serenity concomitant with the state of peace. However, they are here presented in a somewhat more exotic light. They are, in fact, bodhisattvas disguised as arhats.

In earlier sections of this book mention was made of bodhisattvas such as Avalokiteshvara and Manjushri. They are to be distinguished by how the Sixteen Arhats are presented. Whereas these bodhisattvas are depicted as tricosmic figures transcending the bounds of time and space, the arhats are said to be human disciples of the historical Buddha Shakyamuni who achieved sainthood during their lifetimes; and whereas the bodhisattvas were around in the ages of previous buddhas, and will be here until samsara is emptied in order to fulfill their vows of universal responsibility, the arhats have a much more specific agenda.

The bodhisattvas come and go through the pages of history, manifesting in whatever form is best suited to elevate and evolve mankind, taking up and dropping bodily incarnations like a traveler passing through many lands changes his clothing to suit the culture and climate of wherever he may be. The Sixteen Arhats, on the other hand, are disciples of the Buddha who achieved the state of immortality, and will remain in their physical bodies until their purposes have been served. They live quietly and incognito in various places of the world today, performing magical deeds for the benefit of the world, and awaiting the time when they are destined to emerge and play a more significant role. In the meantime, those who pray to and meditate upon them can acquire visions of and teachings directly from them, and can mysteriously receive their blessings.

Although many disciples received arhatship under the Buddha's tutorage, the sixteen came together as a group of specials among equals in the literature and devotional practices of the early Indian Mahayana

writers because of their extraordinary decision to manifest the power of immortality. They are mentioned in the writings of the early Indian master Nandimitra, for example, and also appear in Chinese literature from as early as the seventh century.

Their widespread popularity in Tibet is attributable to the Indian master Atisha, the eleventh-century forefather of the Kadampa school. A text that he wrote on them is preserved in the Tibetan canon. From his time onward, all sects of Tibetan Buddhism incorporated liturgical practices focusing on the Sixteen Arhats, although they received special attention within the Sakya school. Liturgies on them have been composed by such illustrious personages as the First Panchen Lama, the Fifth Dalai Lama, and the Thirteenth Dalai Lama.

Paintings of the Sixteen Arhats often include several other figures, such as the four kingly protectors of the four directions—Dhritarashtra, Virudhaka, Virupaksha, and Vaishravana—and also two assistants—Dharmatala and Hva-shang. We will see more on these six figures later in the treatments of the individual paintings.

Our set of the Sixteen Arhats dates from the mid-1700s, and is painted in the Gadri style, which achieved full maturity in that period. Tibetan paintings in this genre demonstrate a strong Chinese influence in the landscape, which has a subtle and spacious character, and a distinct approach to perspective. The pastel coloring and the shading technique were integrated by Tibetan artists from Chinese paintings of the Ming period (1368–1644).

The brocade frames on the tangkas are the originals, and thus also date from the mid-1700s.

A unique feature of the Sixteen Arhats is that each of them is said to have vowed to remain in his human body on this earth in order to prepare the world for the coming of Buddha Maitreya, the future universal teacher who will usher in a golden age. When the Dharma that was taught by Buddha Shakyamuni is just about to die out, the Sixteen Arhats will come out of their places of retreat, gather together whatever written teachings of the Buddha still survive, and place these inside a stupa made of the seven precious jewels. They will then sit in a circle around the stupa in prayer; their physical bodies will dissolve into light and melt into the stupa, leaving no trace whatsoever behind. The written teachings that are contained in the stupa will later be brought out and become instrumental in bringing in the golden age.

It is believed that each arhat presently has his own dwelling place in the world, as well as his own physical attributes, retinue, and function. Each embodies a specific spiritual quality, and plays a special role in the spiritual world.

There are various ways of listing (and thus portraying) the sixteen, depending on the liturgical tradition on which the paintings of them are based. Ours follows the classical Gelukpa tradition.

Occasionally one sees all Sixteen Arhats depicted in a single tangka, with the Buddha being placed in the center and the arhats gathered around him in a circle. It is more common, however, to find them as a set of paintings, with the size of the set ranging from anywhere between three and nineteen. When this is done, the arhats and their two assistants are distributed accordingly between the different paintings. The set of seven (as in our exhibit) is the most popular.

Here the tangka of Buddha and his two chief disciples serves as the centerpiece to the set, with three paintings being placed to either side of it. The heads of the figures in the three tangkas to Buddha's right face left, and thus inward toward the Buddha; the heads of the figures in the tangkas to Buddha's left face right, and thus also as though looking in at the Buddha. The two assistants—Hva-shang and Dharmatala—are always depicted in the tangkas on the very outside of the set, as though they were watching over everything from the perimeter of the gathering.

The Sixteen Arhats: Painting One

Size: 16″ by 23″
Date: Mid-1700s

Buddha Shakyamuni, who lived 2,500 years ago, is depicted with his two chief Mahayana disciples, Shariputra and Maudgalyayana. All three are dressed in the simple robes of a monk, although these have been richly decorated with golden embellishments. The throne has a brocade hanging with a Dharma wheel on it, indicating that Buddha is in the act of teaching. His right hand is in the mudra of calling the earth as witness to his presence, and his left is in the mudra of meditation.

His halo radiates with a golden light, and has six animals blazing forth from its perimeters. These symbolize his fulfillment of the six paramitas, or perfections: generosity, self-discipline, patience, joyous energy, meditation, and wisdom. Here the elephant stands for generosity, the lion for discipline, the man on the unicorn for patience, the crocodile for joyous energy, the naga holding up jewels for meditation, and the phoenix with a snake in its beak for wisdom.

The throne is upheld by the eight lions of fearlessness in teaching, with two lions on each of the four sides. In front of it we see an arrangement of various offerings. These include the seven royal offerings: elephant tusks, rhino horns, coral, the flaming jewel, the earrings of a king, the earrings of a queen, and a measuring instrument. Eloquent vases hold up flowers in bloom, to symbolize the blossoming of the Dharma.

Buddha's two chief Mahayana disciples, Shariputra and Maudgalyayana. stand to either side of him. They carry the alms bowl and staff characteristic of the monkhood, and seem to be listening attentively to the teaching that the Buddha is giving.

Shariputra is remembered in Buddhist literature as a monk who asked the most questions of the Buddha on the doctrine of voidness, and who thus inspired the Buddha's "Perfection of Wisdom" discourses. Maudgalyayana is remembered as Buddha's foremost disciple in the realm of magical abilities and clairvoyant powers.

The Indian gods Indra and Brahma kneel in front of the Buddha and hold up offerings to him. Here Indra is depicted as offering the conch shell, which represents the sound of the pure Dharma teaching; and Brahma offers a golden Dharma wheel, which represents the eightfold path to enlightenment.

The landscape and foliage in the foreground is shown as being very small in size, in order to magnify the impact of the central figures on the viewer's mind. The subtle use of color and the translucence of Buddha's halo are designed to convey an impression of the etheric nature of an enlightened being's physical presence.

The Sixteen Arhats: Painting Two

Size: 16" by 23"
Date: Mid-1700s

This painting is remarkably preserved, with only slight water damage in the center. A sense of spaciousness is created by the stylization of the lake and by the emerging rocks and mountains in the background. The effect of sunlight playing on a mountain peak in the rear right of the painting is created with gold paint. The size of the trees gives the impression of space and distance.

Arhat Panthaka sits at the top of the composition, and holds up a Buddhist scripture wrapped in a yellow cloth. Next to him, standing on a table, are two flower vases, a *torma* (ritual offering cake), and a small conch shell filled with water, to represent the power of wisdom and the self-confidence and stability that wisdom brings. Holding the text in both hands signifies the manner in which wisdom impacts all dimensions of one's life and actions. The wandering mendicant in front of him holds up a pot filled with food, and has a vase attached to his staff; this symbolizes how wisdom brings both physical and spiritual satiation, and fulfills all needs.

Arhat Kanakavastu sits below him, his hands gently holding one end of a golden chain. The other end of the chain is held by a naga, or mythical water spirit that is half human and half snake. Holding the chain is symbolic of the power of mindfulness, which gives inner peace and mental control. The presence of the naga represents balance and harmony with nature, and also how all the forces of nature contribute to the well-being of one who has inner peace. The arhat and the naga both holding the chain signify how this arhat leads sentient beings out of worldly existence to the spacious realm of nirvana.

Virupaksha, the directional guardian of the west, stands below, his body red in color. He holds a stupa in his left hand, to symbolize the stabilizing power of wisdom.

A row of precious jewels, elephant tusks, and various other royal offerings are set out on the ground below, with a bundle of silk brocades to the side. Wish-fulfilling jewels float up from the waters of the lake. Again, this signifies the prosperity that comes to those who live by spiritual values.

The Sixteen Arhats: Painting Three

Size: 16″ by 23″
Date: Mid-1700s

This painting shows some water damage, but generally is in excellent condition, given its age. The mountains in the background, combined with the rich foliage to the side, give an impression of solitude and quiet meditation.

The Arhat Nagasena is seated at the top of the composition. He holds a monk's staff in his left hand, symbolic of his work to uphold the monastic tradition, and also of arising from the sleep of ignorance. In his right he holds a vase from which rainbow lights shine forth, symbolizing the prosperity that spontaneously comes to those who practice the spiritual path. An attendant, wearing a Tibetan fur hat and Chinese silk robes, stands in front of him and holds up a bowl of fresh fruit.

Below him on the left of the painting is Arhat Abheda. He holds a stupa in his hand, blessing his monk attendant by touching him with the stupa on the forehead. This symbolizes how practice of the spiritual path brings the enlightenment state of the Dharmakaya wisdom.

In the lower right corner stands the directional guardian of the north, known as Vaishravana, his body golden in color. He, like the other three directional guardians, is dressed in the armor of a high-ranking warrior. He holds an umbrella in his right hand, symbolizing protection from the elements, while in his left hand he cradles a mongoose that is spitting out wish-fulfilling jewels, to signify the wealth and prosperity that follows from right living.

❁

The Sixteen Arhats: Painting Four

Size: 16″ by 23″
Date: Mid-1700s

This tangka is an excellent example of the sense of balance, spaciousness, and delicacy achieved by the Gadri style of Tibetan painting, with the white mountains in the background fading into a light blue sky and pale green clouds rolling in from the right. The small hills in the foreground give the impression that the group of arhats and their attendants are in a lost valley far from mundane civilization, yet are working diligently for the benefit of the world.

The dark-skinned Arhat Bakula sits in the back amid a garden of flowers. In his hands he holds a white mongoose spitting wish-fulfilling jewels, the symbol of prosperity and material well-being. His attendant seems to be collecting the jewels, to distribute them among mankind. Thus he symbolizes freedom from spiritual poverty, ignorance, and bondage.

Arhat Gopaka sits to his right, the pages of a scripture in his left hand, while his right shows the mudra of teaching the Dharma. He is one of the few Arhats in this series of paintings who has a mustache. His monk attendant also holds a page of the scripture, and listens to the discourse. Thus he symbolizes the wealth of spiritual learning and the awakening power of wisdom.

Arhat Chudapanthaka sits to Bakula's left, his hands in the meditation posture, a rich blue robe wrapped around his body. He symbolizes success in meditation and inner development. Prayer to him removes the inner and outer obstacles to meditation. His monk attendant is cleaning and polishing his alms bowl, to signify how those who dwell in remote meditation hermitages will always receive the basic necessities of life and never need fear starvation.

On the bottom left stands Virudhaka, the directional guardian of the south, his body blue in color. He holds a sword, signifying protection from life-threatening dangers.

❀

The Sixteen Arhats: Painting Five

Size: 16″ by 23″
Date: Mid-1700s

The composition of this tangka is somewhat more playful than the earlier pieces in the set, with two elephants romping in the foreground and birds frolicking in couples in the lake below.

Arhat Kanaka Bharadvaja is seen at the top of the painting, his hands in the meditation posture. He is seated on a meditation carpet set in a bed of flowers, with the leaves blossoming around him and his shoes on the ground in front. His attendant is depicted as a young maiden holding up an offering of a flaming jewel on a golden plate. He symbolizes the ability of meditation to pacify physical and mental sufferings.

To his left and slightly below him sits Arhat Rahula, who traveled to the realms of the gods and was given a celestial crown for his work there. He holds their gift in his hands, to signify the glory and splendor of spiritual attainment. The mound on the top of his skull is a sign of great attainment in meditation.

The third arhat in this painting, Pindola Bharadvaja, is depicted with an elderly countenance. In one hand he holds up a begging bowl filled with flowers and food, and in the other he holds a text. These symbolize freedom from both material wants and the constrictions of ignorance. His attendant in front of him also holds a book, signifying the transmission of knowledge from one generation to the next. He sits on a white blanket on a bed of leaves, to symbolize the vastness, beauty, and purity of the Dharma life.

In the right corner stands Dhritarashtra, the directional guardian of the east, his body white in color. He plays a lute, to symbolize harmony in form.

❀

Sixteen Arhats: Painting Six

Size: 16″ by 23″
Date: Mid-1700s

In the background we see a single large snow mountain rising from the depths of the earth into the sky, symbolizing the solidity and also the source of all spiritual knowledge. It is ringed by four clouds, each of a different color, that release the rains of the multifaceted Dharma teaching. Three arhats and their Chinese attendant Hva-shang sit below.

Arhat Angaja is depicted at the top of the composition, seated on a cushion of leaves. He holds a fly whisk in his right hand, symbolic of how meditation removes all obstacles, and an incense burner in his left, symbolic of purification through the sweet smell of pure self-discipline. His attendant also holds a flywhisk, again symbolizing Angaja's function to remove spiritual obstacles for practitioners.

The Arhat Vanavasin sits below him and to his right. He holds a fly whisk in his left hand, while his right is in the mudra of forcefully expelling negative energies. He represents victory over the negative mind, and also the prevention of both natural and manmade harms. His begging bowl sits on the table beside him, as does a butterlamp burning with a smooth flame; the former represents how he provides needs to his devotees, while the latter represents the radiance of wisdom. Two devotees hold up a tray of fruit to him as an offering; one is a yogi, and wears a tiger skin shawl and a skirt made of leaves; the other is a dark-skinned yogini, and wears a cotton skirt with a top made of leaves. These represent the special care that the arhat provides to the lay community of meditators.

The third arhat in the picture is Vajriputa, who holds an elegant fan made from peacock feathers in his left hand, and with his right shows the mudra of forcefully expelling negative energies. Together these two gestures signify purification from hindrances and negative karma. A young monk kneels in front of him and holds up an offering of a bowl filled with gold dust; this represents how he brings freedom and liberation to those who devote themselves to him and follow his teachings.

The dark-skinned figure in the foreground is the attendant Hva-shang, who attached himself to the

arhats when they allegedly visited China. He became popular in Tibet as a sort of Chinese Santa Claus. Several children are shown playing around him; like Saint Nick, he always carried little gifts for children on his travels, and loved to play with them. He is always depicted as chubby, good-humored, and playful, i.e., as the archetypical fat and fun-loving monk. Hva-shang is a proponent of the Mahayana teachings, and his role is to assist the arhats in propagating it.

The Sixteen Arhats: Painting Seven

Size: 16″ by 23″
Date: Mid-1700s

In this composition the mountains are shown in soft relief, with the sharply defined clouds creating a strong contrast with the pale sky that turns to a stronger blue as it rises, in order to establish balance with the coloring given to the arhats' bodies.

The Arhat Ajita sits at the top of the group, his hands in the meditation posture. His body is white in color, and a wild elephant plays in the field beside him. His biography states that he was a master meditator who lived in the jungles in solitary retreat, and that wild animals lived with him contentedly and without fear. Thus he symbolizes the power of meditation to overcome wild and dangerous forces, and the power of love to establish peace. The whiteness of his body signifies his pure self-discipline. He brings special blessings for those cultivating the meditative powers of shamatha and samadhi. The table beside him holds his begging bowl and a vase filled with longevity nectars, a symbol of the sustaining and healing effects of meditation.

Most paintings depict him with his head covered by his robes in Ch'an fashion, but here it is left bare. In addition, here he sits on an orange-colored blanket that is arranged on a bed of large leaves, whereas in most portraits he is shown seated on an antelope skin.

His monk attendant is holding up a scripture for him, to signify that meditation should always be practiced in conjunction with study and learning.

Below and to Arhat Ajita's left sits Arhat Kalika, with his right leg resting on top of his left knee. He holds a pair of golden earrings, for he has returned from the heavenly realms, where he taught to the children of the gods and is bearing the gifts that they gave to him. This symbolizes the spiritual rewards that come from divine efforts; devotion to him brings success in the study and teaching of the Dharma. The rock beside him bears several bundles of silk, and also a white vase with coral; these symbolize the merit that arises from Dharma activities. His monk attendant holds up a vase filled with flowers, and requests him to turn the Dharma wheel; this represents the need for and merit in teaching.

Arhat Bhadra sits at the bottom of the painting, his left hand in the meditation posture and his right raised in the mudra of teaching. A lay disciple is preparing a bowl of fruit for him. This symbolizes the importance of senior sangha members combining their meditation practice with Dharma activities, not only in monasteries, but in the ordinary world. Arhat Bhadra represents the protection of Dharma activity for the common people.

The lay attendant Dharmatala stands in the right lower corner, his pet tiger beside him. The tiger represents the energy of the mind that, once tamed, is easily used as a powerful tool. He holds a whisk and a vase containing longevity nectars.

In the previous painting we saw that Hva-shang was a proponent of the Mahayana teachings, and plays the role of facilitating the arhats in teaching it. Here Dharmatala is said to be a proponent of the Hinayana teaching, with the role of assisting the arhats in propagating it. In that the Hinayana and Mahayana together represent the complete teachings of the Buddha (the Mantrayana is a branch of the Mahayana), this means that together they uphold the complete enlightenment tradition.

Art historians disagree on the sources of these two figures. Hva-shang is certainly of Chinese origin, and is continued in the tradition of the "Laughing Buddha," so commonly seen in Chinatown shops around the world. Dharmatala could be of Indian origin; or, as some have suggested, he could also be the god of travel from the ancient kingdom of Kotan, which lay on the Silk Route to the northwest of Tibet and in its heyday was one of the great Buddhist centers of Asia.

Guhyasamaja

Size: 16″ by 22″
Date: Early 1700s

Guhyasamaja, or "The Secret Assembly," refers to the gathering of the thirty-two deities that constitute the mandala of the *Guhyasamaja Tantra*. The name is also sometimes popularly used to refer to the central figure and his consort, although more technically that Buddha figure is called Vajra Akshobya, or "The Unmoving Diamond Buddha." This painting is somewhat damaged from the rigors of time, but nonetheless is an excellent example of the richness in color used in eighteenth century Tibet. The brocade frame also dates from that period.

The Guhyasamaja mandala represents one of the first in the highest yoga tantra class to surface publicly in India. Scholars such as Alex Wayman, who has written extensively on the subject, date its public emergence to the fourth century A.D. It is also one of the few tantras for which the original Indian Sanskrit texts still survives; with many of the other tantras, the original texts are only extant in Tibetan, Mongolian, or Chinese translation. Many Indian commentaries to the system by such illustrious authors as Nagarjuna, Aryadeva, and Chandrakirti can be found in the Tibetan canon of translated Sanskrit treatises.

According to tradition, the Buddha originally taught the *Guhyasamaja Tantra* to King Indrabhuti, who requested a tantric meditation that he could practice without taking any time off from his ordinary activities. As a ruler of an important kingdom he had many affairs of state to oversee, public responsibilities to fulfill, and five hundred affectionate wives to satisfy. The Buddha taught him Guhyasamaja as a way of living in the mundane world while taking the activities of everyday life as the object of his meditation.

Guhyasamaja is popularly known as *Tantra-raja*, or "King of the Tantras," because it provides an important key to the understanding of the vast reservoir of tantric

literature. It is the principal subject of study in the two Gelukpa tantric colleges: Gyumey and Gyuto. It is said that if one understands the *Guhyasamaja Tantra* one can easily comprehend any other tantric system.

Several lineages of the Guhyasamaja transmission existed in Tibet prior to Tsongkhapa's time. He gathered all of these together, but was especially impressed by the lineage descending from Marpa Lotsawa, the eleventh-century forefather of the Kargyu school, and he made this his main emphasis. Guhyasamaja became Lama Tsongkhapa's principal tantric practice, and the subject of a four-year meditation retreat in the Olkha mountains. Therefore he is depicted in the upper-left hand corner of the painting.

The central deity of the mandala is portrayed as having three faces, one of which is blue, one white, and one red. This symbolizes how in the tantric practice of Guhyasamaja one can use the energy of the three root delusions—apathy, anger, and lust—and transform them into the enlightenment experience.

In general the highest yoga tantras are divided into three types: male, female, and neutral. The first emphasizes the illusory body yoga; the second emphasizes the clear light yoga; and the third presents both yogas in balance. The first is for trainees with predominantly aggressive tendencies, the second for trainees of strong lust, and the third for trainees of strong apathy. Guhyasamaja is the chief of the male tantras, and thus mostly emphasizes aggression and the illusory body doctrine. However, as indicated by the three faces, his practice brings all three distortions into the path.

Various dharmapala adorn the bottom of the tangka, and express their vows to protect practitioners.

On the back of the painting, a large stupa, symbolic of the enlightened mind, has been drawn with dark red ink.

❁

Heruka Chakrasamvara

Size: 18″ by 26″
Date: Late 1800s

This well-preserved painting, which belonged to the previous Dalai Lama, known as the Great Thirteenth, exhibits the form of stylization popular in late nineteenth-century Tibet, with snow mountains, rocks, trees, and flowers presented in bold, slightly heavy lines. The brocade is from a later date. His Holiness the Thirteenth Dalai Lama sealed the painting on the back of the canvas with his handprints in saffron dye.

Heruka Chakrasamvara is the principal highest yoga tantra in the female class of tantras, meaning that it emphasizes using lust as the path to enlightenment, and also emphasizes practice of the clear light yoga. The name translates as "The Wheel of Bliss," for whoever engages in the yogas of the Chakrasamvara system learns to draw all experiences of life into the wheel of pleasure.

The symbolism of Heruka Chakrasamvara is explained as follows. His twelve arms represent the twelve links of interdependent origination, which as an object of meditation leads the practitioner to realization of the nature of the conventional reality of illusory occurrences and the ultimate reality of emptiness. The four faces represent the four enlightenment activities: pacification, increase, power, and wrath. Each face has a slightly different expression that is a combination of wrath and laughter, representing how the expression of enlightenment manifests in accordance with the needs of trainees. The three eyes see everything throughout the three worlds—above, below, and in between—and also have the clairvoyance to see everything in the past, present, and future. The five skulls on his head represent the transformation of the five root delusions into the five wisdoms. The garland of fifty skulls that he wears represents the transformation of the ordinary mindsets into the enlightenment experience. The crescent moon in his hair represents universal love and compassion. His four fangs represent destruction of the four maras, or devils. In this way every detail on his body represents an enlightenment quality that is to be achieved by those who engage in the yogas symbolized by his mandala.

According to the legend, Buddha first taught this tantra as a means of subduing the Hindu tantric cults of India that made living sacrifices as part of their worship of the god Ishvara, who in more recent times is called Shiva. To turn them away from their misguided ways, he manifested as Heruka Chakrasamvara, together with the mandala of sixty-two divinities, and pressed down on Ishvara's palace. Ishvara surrendered, and promised to mend his mistaken ways. This is depicted by the deities upon whom Heruka is dancing. This legend perhaps suggests that the Heruka tantric system is a reexpression of the yogas of the Ishvara tradition, recast in a Buddhist context.

In the upper-right corner Buddha Shakyamuni sits in meditation, for he was the original source of the teaching. Tsongkhapa sits in the clouds in the upper-left corner, for he was the principal Tibetan elucidator of the tradition.

In the bottom left is Palden Lhamo, the goddess of the Oracle Lake and a principal Dharmapala in the Gelukpa school. Vaishravana, the god of prosperity, is in the lower right.

The golden bowl in the lower center of the tangka rests on a tiger skin, for the Indian yogis who popularized the *Chakrasamvara Tantra* in India, such as Krishnacharya, Gandhapada, and Luipa, often lived in jungles and dressed in the skins of wild animals. The bowl contains various offering substances, including torma-offering cakes, fruits, and so forth.

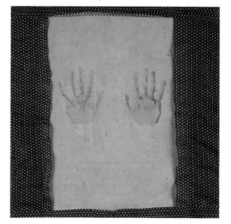

109

Vajrabhairava

Size: 18″ x 26″
Date: Late 1800s

This tangka, also a sacred possession of the Great Thirteenth Dalai Lama, was made by the same artist and in the same style as the previous piece, i.e., that of Heruka Chakrasamvara. The original brocade frame was probably also replaced at the same time.

Guhyasamaja, Heruka Chakrasamvara, and Vajrabhairava are the three main tantric systems practiced in the Gelukpa school. The first emphasizes the illusory body yoga, the second the clear light doctrines, and the third the power of both in balance.

Vajrabhairava literally translates as "The Diamond Terrifier." Another name for him is Yamantaka, or "The Opponent of Death." The sense of the two names is that meditation upon this mandala terrifies and chases away the three kinds of death: outer, inner, and secret. The first is ordinary premature death caused by obstacles; inner death refers to the delusions and spiritual distortions, which kill happiness for self and others; and secret death refers to blockages in the subtle energy channels of the body, which produce an according mental distortion.

Yamantaka is depicted with a buffalo face having two horns; these represent the illusory body and clear light doctrines, the essence of all Buddha's tantric teachings. He has nine heads, because the system incorporates all nine categories of the Buddha's teachings. His thirty-four arms, together with body, speech, and mind, point to the thirty-seven wings of enlightenments. His sixteen legs represent the sixteen aspects of the emptiness doctrine. He stands on eight Hindu gods and eight animals, symbolic of how meditation upon the Yamantaka mandala brings the eight occult powers and eight paranormal abilities. The many implements that he holds signify various aspects of his yogic system. For example, the man skewered on a stick shows how practice of the system brings enlightenment in one lifetime.

Buddha Shakyamuni sits in the upper-right corner, and in the upper left is Rva Lotsawa, the eleventh-century master who brought the lineage to Tibet. On the bottom right we see Kalarupa, who is the Bodhisattva Manjushri, manifest as a dharmapala. On the bottom left is Mahakala, who is the great bodhisattva Avalokiteshvara, manifest as a dharmapala.

Kurukulla

Size: 21″ x 32″
Date: Late 1700s

This is an excellent example of a *tsel-tang*, the style of tangka made by first coating the canvas with red vermillion and then creating fine silhouettes with ink made from gold dust. Thin washes of various colors are then added to create a sense of clouds and other background figures. The outer silk brocade frame is about 120 years old, with the red inner stripe being more recent.

Kurukulla is a female buddha who is considered to be a form of Tara. Tara in general is a symbol of the enlightenment deeds of the buddhas; her form as Kurukulla is especially associated with the expression of that enlightenment energy for stability and success in worldly matters, as well as with magical powers, such as subjugating evil, subduing personal enemies, attracting material wealth, and so forth.

The practice of the Kurukulla mandala was brought to Tibet by Atisha Dipamkara Shrijnana in the mid-eleventh century and was especially popular in the early Kadampa school.

Kurukulla's three eyes represent the clear vision of the conventional and ultimate levels of reality and the paranormal abilities that come to those who meditate upon her mandala. She has four arms for the four immeasurable attitudes: love, compassion, joy in the success of others, and equanimity with all living beings. Two of her hands hold bow and arrow, representing the latent energy and penetrating insight inherent in the practice. In a third hand she holds an iron hook decorated with flowers, indicating how her practice pulls in all magical powers; her fourth hand holds a lasso made from flowers, indicating how her practice is a sweet yet firm method in fulfilling both temporal or spiritual goals.

In the top center of the painting we see Buddha Amitabha, an indication that Kurukulla belongs to the Lotus Family of tantric practices. Of the several figures below her, one is the great Indian master Nagarjuna, who propagated the *Kurukulla Tantra* in India. Below him is the mahasiddha Dombhi Heruka, who also propagated the practice in India. He rides on a tiger and has his consort beside him.

Various other gurus in the lineage of transmission watch over the central figure.

There are three forms of Kurukulla—outer, inner, and secret—and all three are depicted in the tangka. The outer form is set as the central figure of the composition, as described above. The inner form is in the bottom-left corner, and is seen dancing on a sun disk which is above a human body; she is surrounded by various deities, such as the wealth god Jambala, Nagaraja, and a form of Mahakala. Her secret form is seen in the right bottom, surrounded by dakinis, and by various deities symbolizing worldly powers, such as Kalarati, Bhairava, and Nagaraja.

113

Sacred Text of the *Prajna Paramita Sutra*

Size: 24" x 6"
Date: Early 1900s

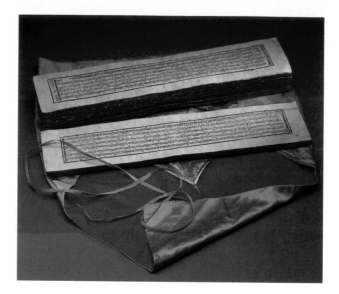

This is a woodblock print of the most popular with Tibetans of Buddha's forty-two *Discourses on the Perfection of Wisdom*, or *Prajna Paramita Sutras*. It is the version in eight thousand verses, and is printed on hand-made wood paper. It was used by His Holiness the Dalai Lama when he first received the transmission of these teachings in his youth, and again many years later when he taught the *Prajna Paramita* to the monks at Drepung Monastery.

The Robe of a Monk
Size: 8' 6" x 3' x 10"

The *cho-goe*, or outer robe worn by a monk at monastic gatherings, teachings, and ceremonial occasions, is made from many pieces of cloth sewn together as a shawl. The *cho-goe* in our exhibit was worn by His Holiness for many years, and is on loan from him.

The patchwork design of the *cho-goe* has its origins in early Indian Buddhism. Buddha Shakyamuni was born into an India with a strong and highly venerated tradition of wandering mendicants. These mendicants were not allowed to own anything other than their robes, a sleeping roll, an alms bowl, a walking staff, and a water filter. In these ancient days a monk was not allowed to have more food than he could consume in a single day, and even then was allowed to eat only once daily. He generally made his robes from pieces of discarded cloth, which were then sewn together and dyed saffron, red, or blue; white and black were disallowed, because white was the color worn by Hindu priests, and black by aristocrats.

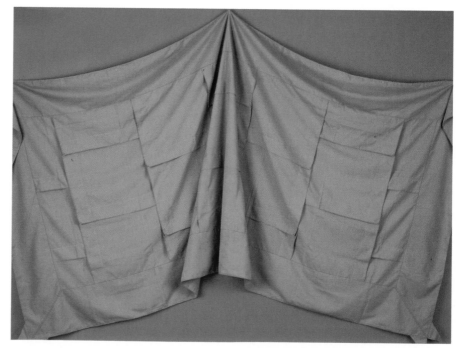

The early Buddhist monks followed this extremely austere tradition. However, with the passage of time, the lifestyle lost its venerability in the eyes of the masses, and monks became expected to lead more organized and stable lives. This had already occurred in India by the time Buddhism came to Tibet.

Robes were no longer sewn together from pieces of rags. Instead, the ancient legacy was honored by sewing the upper robe in a patchwork design, symbolic of the intense renunciation that the early Indians had practiced.

A Set of Ritual Implements

A number of ritual implements are used in daily meditation by His Holiness. They include a vajra and bell set (5″ long and 7″ high, respectively) that date back to the Fourth Dalai Lama (1589–1617). In tantric rituals the vajra is held in the right hand, to symbolize transforming aggressive male energy into compassion, and the bell is held in the left, to symbolize transforming female intuitive energy into wisdom.

To its right sits a hand drum (3.5″ wide by 2″ thick), known as a *damaru*. Drums of this nature are sometimes made of two human skulls bonded together and covered with human skin; this one is made of ivory and has ordinary sheepskin. It belonged to the previous Dalai Lama. When played, it is held in front of the navel with the right hand, to represent the power of controlling the kundalini energy.

On the outside left is a kapala, or inner offering vessel, made of gilded silver (9″ high). The liquid inside It is called "the inner offering" because the liquids that it contains represent the transformation of the five aspects of one's beings into the five buddha qualities, and of the five delusions into the five wisdoms. It is in the shape of a cup made from a human skull, to represent the impermanence of the human condition.

A mantra rosary made of 112 carnelian beads sits in the front. Every tantric sadhana, or daily meditation practice, includes a phase involving mantra recitation. The rosary is used as a counter; the practitioner commits himself to reciting a set number of "rounds" of mantras each day. In formal retreats the meditator determines to complete hundreds of thousands, and sometimes even millions, of mantra recitations.

Butterlamp

Height: 5″

The butterlamp is another item set on the altar of a practicing Buddhist for the offering of light. In Tibet the vessel would be filled with the butter of a dri, or female counterpart of the yak. A cotton wick is placed in the center of the vessel, and fresh butter added every few hours. On auspicious occasions Tibetans offer thousands of butterlamps in their temples and monasteries. His Holiness used this lamp on his alter for many years.

Amulet

Size: 7.5″ high by 5.5″ in diameter
Date: Mid-1800s

The *gaou*, or amulet box, is a kind of portable altar used by Tibetans, and usually contains blessing substances, an image of a holy being, such as a guru, buddha, or bodhisattva, protection mantras, and sometimes even medicines. This *gaou* is an excellent example of Tibetan metal craftsmanship, with the front-piece bearing engravings of the three main bodhisattvas—Avalokiteshvara (on top), Manjushri (left), and Vajrapani (right), representing the compassion, wisdom, and strength of the enlightened mind.

Traditionally the window of the *gaou* reveals the face of a small metal, clay, or wooden statue. On ours we see the introduction of a more modern element: a photograph of the late Kyabjey Trijang Rinpochey, the younger of the two principal lamas who educated His Holiness the Dalai Lama.

At the bottom of the *gaou* is an engraving of the image known as "The Long Lived," which is made up of six auspicious elements: a bird, a deer, an old man, a tree, a rock, and a waterfall. Most Tibetan households have a depiction of this sixfold theme somewhere on the premises.

SECTION TWO:

SACRED OBJECTS FROM
DREPUNG LOSELING MONASTERY

Two Lineage Trees

The first two items in the selection of artworks from the surviving archives of Drepung Loseling are known as *tsok-shing*, or "assembly trees." Here the word "assembly" has two meanings: the images on the paintings are an assembly of the historical personages in the important lineages of transmission, as well as of the major divinities that embody the sentiment of these lineages; and also the practitioner assembles or collects great merit and wisdom by meditating on these images.

Both of the "assembly tree" images are Gelukpa; that is to say, they depict the principal lineages of transmission of which the Gelukpa school is comprised, as well as the divinities held in highest esteem within the Gelukpa. Most Gelukpa monks cultivate a daily meditation practice focusing on one of these two images, in which the visualization is created, prayers chanted, and so forth. The first is used mainly by younger monks, and the second by elder ones, who have received tantric initiation.

The Lam Rim Assembly Tree

Size: 22″ by 32″
Date: Early 1900s

The Tibetan name for this tangka, *Lam Rim Tsokshing*, translates as "Assembly Tree of the Stages on the Path of Tradition." It depicts the principal Indian and Tibetan masters and divinities associated with the transmission of the Lam Rim, or "Stages on the Path" teaching, a code name for the manner in which the Indian master Atisha Dipamkara Shrijnana, the eleventh-century founder of the Kadampa school, structured the exoteric or Sutrayana teachings of the Buddha. As was stated in Part One, Atisha's presentation later became the principal building block in Tsongkhapa's Gelukpa Order, as well as an important element in all schools of Tibetan Buddhism.

There are three ways to depict the Lam Rim Assembly Tree: extensive, medium, and abbreviated. This is the abbreviated form, in which only the most famous masters and most popular divinities are included.

In the center we see Buddha Shakyamuni, with a small image of his tantric aspect as Buddha Vajradhara at his heart. This indicates that the exoteric Sutrayana practices taught by the Buddha and arranged into the Lam Rim tradition are used primarily preliminary to entering into the esoteric tantric training.

Surrounding the Buddha we see four clusters of figures: one to his right (the viewer's left), one to his left, one in front, and one behind (depicted as though above). Those to the right and left depict respectively the lineage holders in the two main aspects of the Buddha's teachings, which are known as "The Lineage of Extensive Bodhisattva Activities" and "The Lineage of the Profound View." The clusters behind and in front depict respectively the main lineages of tantric transmission and the principal divinities that are worshipped in the Gelukpa.

"The Lineage of Extensive Bodhisattva Activities" refers to the general teachings of the Buddha, both Hinayana and Mahayana, on the stages of discipline, meditation, conduct, and so forth. These were compiled by the bodhisattva Maitreya and passed to the Indian master Asanga, who arranged them into "The Five Treatises of Maitreya," which form the approach to this aspect of Buddha's teachings. The lineage then passed through many generations of Indian masters, until they came to Atisha, who brought them to Tibet. After that they were transmitted in Tibet through a dozen generations of early Kadampa lamas and came to Tsongkhapa. From Tsongkhapa's time onward they have been passed through a line of Gelukpa masters.

"The Lineage of the Profound View" refers to the aspect of Buddha's teachings that deal with specifically the doctrine of emptiness and the two levels of reality—ultimate and conventional—and how these co-exist simultaneously. These teachings were transmitted by the bodhisattva Manjushri, who gave them to the Indian master Nagarjuna. Nagarjuna compiled them into his famous "Six Treatises on Knowledge," which became the basis of the tradition. After that they passed through many generations of Indian masters until they came to Atisha, who brought them to Tibet. For four centuries in Tibet they were passed through the Kadampa lamas, and finally came to Tsongkhapa. From that time onward they have been transmitted through Gelukpa lamas.

Thus, in both of these clusters of gurus, we have three phases of transmission: the early Indian masters; the early Kadampa lamas; and then the Gelukpa lamas.

Behind the Buddha (here shown above) is Buddha Vajradhara and the lineage holders of the "Blessed Tantric Practice Transmission," meaning the various lineages of Vajrayana transmissions. Here only a few figures are depicted, as this tangka is the abbreviated version.

In front of and below the Buddha are rows of various categories of divinities. The first row contains tantric meditational deities, or *Yidams*. The second row contains ten buddhas, to represent the buddhas of the ten directions (i.e., all enlightened beings).

The third row shows the main bodhisattvas, such as Arya Tara, Manjusri, Vajrapani, and so forth, who represent all bodhisattvas. The fourth row shows the type of arhats known as pratyekabuddhas, recognizable by the protrusions on the top of their heads. The fifth row depicts the type of arhat known as sravakas, to which the Sixteen Arhats belong. The sixth row has dakas and dakinis, flanked by the two assistants to the Sixteen Arhats, Dharmatala and Hva-shang. Finally, the bottom row shows the wrathful dharmapalas.

The entire assembly is supported on branches and leaves of a tree that grows out of the earth, to indicate the organic nature of the lineage of transmission, i.e., that the enlightenment experience is passed from generation to generation in a naturally unfolding way.

The four directional guardians sit below the tree, as do the Hindu gods Indra and Brahma. The fact that they are below and not on the tree indicates that they are unenlightened beings and not part of the transmission; yet their presence in the composition shows they are regarded with respect and are seen as highly evolved and powerful beings who support and protect the transmission.

As said above, this image is used in visualization as part of a daily liturgy by monks of the Gelukpa school as a preliminary to silent meditation. When this is done, all the principal names of the lineage gurus are chanted, with a prayer to them and the various divinities for their blessings in the quest to accomplish realization of the path. This is followed by Lam Rim–style meditation, after which all the elements of the tree dissolve into the Buddha, who shrinks to the size of one's thumb and comes to the center of one's heart, where he remains until the next meditation session, symbolizing that one's body, speech, and mind become of one nature with the body, speech, and mind of the Buddha and the assembly.

❁

Lama Chopa Assembly Tree

Size: 26" by 37"
Date: Early 1900s

The Tibetan name for this tangka is *Lama Chopa Tsokshing*, which translates as "The Assembly Tree of the Guru Devotion Practice." Many elements of it are similar to those of the Lam Rim Assembly Tree, the main difference being that here there is a stronger focus on the tantric element.

Lama Chopa, which means "Guru Devotion," is the name of a liturgical text written by the First Panchen Lama in the mid-seventeenth century that since then has been chanted daily by almost every adult monk in the Gelukpa school. This painting is a map to the visualization done in conjunction with that liturgy.

The image itself has many elements in common with the previous tangka, i.e., the Lam Rim Assembly Tree, although this is a more expanded version and thus has many more figures on it.

Again, the clusters to the right and left of the central figure represent the transmission gurus respectively in the Lineage of Extensive Bodhisattva Activities and the Lineage of Profound View. Here again we see the three periods in the transmission: the early Indian masters; the early Kadampa lamas; and then the Gelukpa masters.

Above the central image are five lines of gurus. In visualization these are actually behind the central figure. These are the five principal tantric lineages practiced in the Gelukpa, each of which is identifiable by the figure at the top of the line. From the viewer's right these are: Guhyasamaja, Vajrabhairava, Vajradhara, Manjushri, and Heruka Chakrasamvara. Earlier we saw tangkas of Guhyasamaja, Vajrabhairava, and Heruka Chakrasamvara, the three main Gelukpa Yidams. Here Vajradhara in the center does not represent a Yidam as such, but is a general symbol for all tantric Yidams other than the three explicitly presented. Manjushri also does not here represent a Yidam as such, but rather symbolizes the special tantric transmission of *mahamudra*, or the emptiness doctrine, as practiced within the Gelukpa.

The central figure resembles Lama Tsongkhapa, the founder of the Gelukpa Order, but in fact is one's own principal guru as an embodiment of the various lineages of transmission and divinities depicted in the composition. All these lineages came to Tsongkhapa, as did the practices of all the divinities that are depicted in the composition.

Below the central figure are the various categories of divinities. Because this is the extensive version of the image, each of the four classes of tantras is given its own row for the deities belonging to it, beginning with the highest yoga tantra deities in the top row. As in the Lam Rim Assembly Tree, below them are rows respectively for the buddhas, bodhisattvas, pratyekabuddha arhats, shravaka arhats, dakas and dakinis, and finally dharmapalas. Again, all of this rests on branches and leaves of a tree, symbolizing the pure and beyond-samsara nature of the assembly. Below the tree are the four directional protectors and various Hindu gods, who worship and support the enlightenment masters and their tradition.

The daily Lama Chopa practice belongs to the category of devotions known as guru yoga. One visualizes the Assembly Tree, visualizes making offerings, chants verses of praise and homage, and requests blessings for the accomplishment of quick realization. The entire assembly then dissolves into the central figure, who comes to the crown of one's head, shrinks to the size of one's thumb, and melts into one's body, where he comes to the center of one's heart. One's own body, speech, and mind thus become one with the body, speech, and mind of the guru.

❈

Vajrayogini

Size: 22" by 34"
Date: Early 1900s

This tangka depicts the mandala palace of the three main forms of Vajrayogini, the highest yoga tantra deity, who is the consort of Heruka Chakrasamvara.

The central figure is known in Tibetan as *Naro Khachomo* (see page 135), which means "The Space Dancer of Naropa." She is given this name because her lineage descends from the eleventh-century Indian mahasiddha Naropa, and also because she is the queen of the Paradise of Dakinis, where the beings have the power of levitation and flight. One of the side-effects of her practice is the ability to levitate. This form of Vajrayogini is practiced mostly in the Sakya and Gelukpa schools.

To the right of her is another Vajrayogini form, known as Vajravarahi, which is practiced mainly in the twelve Kargyupa sects. The third form of Vajrayogini—here depicted as being surrounded by a rainbow—is practiced mostly in the Nyingma tradition, and brings the power to melt one's body into rainbow light at the time of death and take it with one to the Dakini lands.

Behind the inner walls of the palace, manifestations of Vajrayogini's body mandala dance on an exquisitely tiled floor. A lotus bearing an offering bowl grows out of a pond located in the center of the inner courtyard, with a sacrificial offering rising from it. Sixteen goddesses of various colors dance outside the outer wall and display a range of offerings. Offering dakas and dakinis hover in the top corners of the painting.

The bottom row of the painting contains various wrathful protectors. In the left corner are the Skeleton Lords known as Sitapatti, who are dharmapalas specific to this tantra.

The lineage holders of the tradition float in the sky above the palace, forming a direct link between the masters of the past and the present generation of practitioners.

The composition also includes the three principal Gelukpa mandala deities: Guhyasamaja, Heruka Chakrasamvara, and Vajrabhairava. Guhyasamaja is in the upper-left corner, Vajrabhairava in the upper-right, and Heruka Chakrasamvara in the attic under the golden roof.

125

Ushnisha Sitatapatra

Size: 18.5″ by 26″
Date: early 1800s

The name Ushnisha Sitatapatra translates as "The Victorious White Parasol." Her parasol indicates her ability to protect sentient beings from natural catastrophes, diseases, and so forth. She is white in color, because the principal means by which she accomplishes this function is the enlightenment energy of pacification.

Ushnisha Sitatapatra is a female form of Avalokiteshvara, the Bodhisattva of Compassion. Like him in his elaborate form, she also has a thousand eyes that watch over living beings, and a thousand arms that protect and assist them. Thus she symbolizes the power of active compassion.

Her faces are stacked up in the form of the mandala of the five Buddha families, with the according colors: white, yellow, red, green, and blue. This represents the ability of her yogas to transform the five delusions—attachment, aversion, jealousy, pride, and ignorance—into the five wisdoms.

While her left hand graciously supports a white parasol, her right holds a small Dharma wheel, symbolizing how meditation upon her brings all spiritual knowledge. Her feet dance upon numerous types of gods, spirits, and animals, for she brings control over all natural forces.

Lama Tsongkhapa, flanked by his two main disciples, sits in the sky above, for the lineage of the practice descends through them.

On the bottom of the composition is the Lion-Headed Dakini, known in Tibetan as Sengdongma. She represents the bold and fearless nature of wisdom. The dharmapala Kalarupa and his consort dance beside her, protecting practitioners from obstacles and negative forces.

✿

Pehar

Size: 16″ by 22.5″
Date: Mid-1600s

The main figure in the composition is the six-armed protector Pehar, a dharmapala that was brought to Tibet by Guru Padma Sambhava in the mid-eighth century and appointed by him to serve as the protector deity of Samyey, Tibet's first monastery, and to work for its prosperity and success. Pehar is also the chief dharmapala of Drepung Loseling Monastery.

Pehar is also a deity that is channeled by several oracular mediums in Tibet, the most famous being at Nechung Monastery, which was located beside Drepung near Lhasa. The Nechung medium has served as the State Oracle of Tibet since the time of the Fifth Dalai Lama, and Pehar's advice is sought in all important matters of state, as well as in the search for all Dalai Lama reincarnations.

The unique connection between Pehar and the Dalai Lamas was first established during the lifetime of the second incarnation, and according to legend took a paranormal turn after his death in 1542. He was considering not reincarnating in Tibet, for he found the Tibetans disconcertingly quarrelsome. Guru Padma Sambhava, Atisha, and Tsongkhapa all appeared to him in his after-death experience, and requested he change his mind. Guru Padma Sambhava prophesied that if he were to agree to continue working in Tibet an event would occur after a hundred years in which he would be put in a position to bring peace and stability to the Land of Snows and secure the enlightenment tradition for hundreds of years to come. Padma Sambhava appointed Pehar as his special assistant in this work.

Consequently, the Second reincarnated in Tibet, and eventually was enthroned as the Third Dalai Lama. During his lifetime he brought the Mongolians to Buddhism and thus tamed their war-like ways. Then, during his incarnation as the Great Fifth, Tibet erupted in a civil war, and after the dust cleared he was appointed as temporal and spiritual leader of the Tibetan nation. This occurred in 1642, exactly a hundred years after Padma Sambhava's prophecy.

Pehar has remained the main assistant divinity to the Dalai Lamas in their work as national chieftain of the Tibetan people ever since that time.

The Fifth Dalai Lama, Losang Gyatso, is depicted in the upper-right corner of the tangka. All the deities in the tangka are associated with practices popular with the Great Fifth, meaning that it probably belonged to one of his close disciples.

A six-armed form of Hayagriva stands at the top of the tangka, his body red in color. He is Amitabha, the Buddha of Boundless Light, in the form of a wrathful meditational deity, and was one of the Great Fifth's principal mandala practices, as well as one of the main traditions associated with Samyey Monastery over the centuries.

In front of Pehar and slightly to his right, the female protector Palden Lhamo rides a donkey through a lake of blood, while the red protector Begtsey dances with a sword and a human heart in his hands. Palden Lhamo is the goddess of the Oracle Lake and a special protectress of the Dalai Lamas since the time of the First; Begtsey is the dharmapala especially linked to the *Hayagriva Tantra* and was a special protector of the Fifth Dalai Lama.

The landscape in the background depicts birds in flight carrying human entrails in their beaks, symbolizing the impermanence of things and also the manner in which the practice devours all negativity. The table in front has a tripod of three small human skulls holding up a larger skull filled with human eyes, ears, brain, nose, and tongue; this is an offering of the five senses in wrathful form.

This is the oldest painting in the exhibt and reflects the exquisite brush work of the Tibetan artists of the seventeenth century. It is the type of tangka known in Tibetan as *nak-thang*, in which the artist first covers the canvas with black paint and then works on top of this with gold. The technique is reserved mostly for Dharma Protectors and wrathful Yidams. The black color is made from a concoction of lamp soot and indigo, thus giving it a slightly bluish tint. Various mineral colors are used to shade the bodies of the deities in order to provide a sense of depth.

129

Lama Tsongkhapa

Size: 2′ 8″ high
Date: Mid-1400s

This exquisite image, made of gilded bronze, was commissioned by Chieftain Ganden Tsewang of Gugey in 1423 and offered to Ganden Chokhor, one of Drepung Loseling's affiliate monasteries in western Tibet. It served as the central image in that temple until the monastery was destroyed in 1959.

A special feature of the early images of Tsongkhapa is that they are less stylized than later creations, and thus resemble his actual appearance more accurately. A glance at some of the tangkas in which Tsongkhapa appears demonstrates this.

The overhead banner, which represents his halo, was made at a later date, probably a century or so after the image itself. The six animals in it—two elephants, two snow lions, two unicorns, two crocodiles, two nagas, and a garuda at the top—represent the fulfillment and complete maturity of the six perfections: generosity, self-discipline, patience, joyous energy, meditation, and wisdom. A royal umbrella crowns the top of the halo, symbolic of the harmony and glory of the enlightenment experience.

Buddha Maitreya

Size: 33″ high
Date: Late 1500s

Just as Christians await the coming of Christ, Buddhists throughout the world await the coming of Buddha Maitreya. He is prophesied to become the fifth universal teacher of this world era. His deeds will usher in a golden age on earth, and bring an end to the culture of war, violence, intolerance, and hatred that characterizes the present time in human history. Those who meditate upon him will be reborn then and help in the work of creating the new age.

Maitreya is a favorite subject of artists in the Gelukpa school. Tsongkhapa named his monastery after Maitreya's pure land paradise, which is called Tushita in Sanskrit, a term that was translated into Tibetan as Ganden; early Gelukpa lamas were called Gandenpas because of this strong connection. The name Maitreya literally translates as "Love"; its Tibetan counterpart, Champa, is one of the most common personal names of Gelukpa monks.

Although here Maitreya appears in the form of a bodhisattva, this is just a piece of theater and an illusory drama that he performs for the sake of tradition. When he incarnates as the man destined to play the role of the fifth universal teacher, he will go through the motions of birth, training, meditation, and the attainment of enlightenment; but in reality he is already a buddha, and just pretends to accomplish these deeds in order to benefit the minds of trainees.

Maitreya's hands are in the teaching mudra, for he presently resides as the Lord of Tushita Pure Land, where he teaches to those who are reborn there while awaiting his prophesied time to descend to earth (see page 159). The facial expression on the image portrays him as youthful and loving, for he has achieved the state of eternal youth, and as a bodhisattva thinks only of how to benefit sentient beings.

Images of Maitreya often depict a stupa in the hairpiece. According to legend, Maitreya Buddha adopted this as his logo in recognition of the work of his predecessor, Buddha Shakyamuni. Also, it symbolizes how the force of love, of which Maitreya is the embodiment, leads to certain buddhahood.

This particular statue of Maitreya is made of gilded copper. It was constructed in pieces and then assembled. The joining rivets are quite visible and exemplify an important sixteenth-century technique of sculpture.

Most ornaments on the image, like the armlets and the crown, have been made separately and embody a high degree of ornamentation. The large aura is attached to the body by a thin wire. The crown is delicately sculpted and adorned with turquoise, jade, and other semi-precious jewels.

❀

Vajrayogini

Size: 22"
Date: Late 1500s

This image, known as *Naro Khachoma*, or "Naropa's Space Dancer," represents one of the three main forms of Vajrayogini practiced in Tibet, and the main form of the deity propitiated within the Gelukpa school. The lineage passed from the Indian mahasiddha Naropa to the Pamtingpa brothers in the eleventh century, who brought it to Tibet. In Tibet it was propagated in the early Sakya school, and came into the Gelukpa from them.

Vajrayogini is the consort of Heruka Chakrasamvara, and thus her practice is a simplification of the *Heruka-Tantra*. Most Tibetan temples contain an image of one of the numerous Vajrayogini forms. The practice is especially associated with the use of sexual energy for enlightenment, and the transformation of ordinary passion into wisdom. It works with the blissful kundalini energies of the body, mastery of which brings paranormal physical powers, such as levitation, walking through solid matter, and so forth.

Vajrayogini is seen as having a naked sixteen-year old body, to symbolize freedom from ordinary conceptions. In paintings and visualization her body is seen as red in color, representing the bliss of the inner heat that is generated when passion transforms into compassion. The three eyes symbolize her ability to see past, present, and future simultaneously. Her eyes gaze upwards, indicating her power to guide practitioners directly to enlightenment. In her right hand, she holds a curved knife, symbolic of the wisdom that cuts through ignorance; and in her left she raises a skull cup filled with blood, symbolizing the blissful consciousness that gives rise to wisdom. Her bone ornaments symbolize the first five of the six perfections—generosity, discipline, patience, effort, and meditation—while her naked body represents the sixth perfection, i.e., that of wisdom. A garland of fifty skulls hangs around her neck, indicating that her practice causes the ordinary mindsets to transform into pure wisdom; but unlike most images of highest yoga tantra, where the heads are freshly severed and dripping with blood, here the skulls are without any flesh and are "dry," representing the fierceness of the inner-heat yoga associated with her practice, which dries up all mental distortions.

A khatvanga staff rests over her left shoulder, representing the presence of her male partner Heruka Chakrasamvara and indicating their inseparability. The symbolism of the khatvanga is in itself very profound, and each detail can be understood as representing different aspects of their mandala of sixty-two deities. She is standing on the worldly gods Bhairava and Kalarati, who according to one tradition symbolize the hatred and attachment to be overcome by following this practice. In another version, Bhairava stands for the energy and Kalarati the wisdom aspect of this tantra.

According to oral tradition, this particular image is one of the most holy yogini statues in the monastery, and frequently speaks directly to practitioners. Tibetans believe that a statue or painting can acquire this extraordinary characteristic, for the enlightened beings actually reside in them. Some statues are said to move, walk, dance, and so forth.

The image is an excellent example of the quality of metalwork achieved by Tibetan artists. The wooden base is from a later date, as is the flaming halo.

The image is decorated with various jewels, such as turquoise, rubies, crystals, and so forth, that have been added by different practitioners over the centuries. This was a common practice with especially holy images. Her body is robed in brocades, with the skirt being fringed with tassels. The top part is shaped like a star, and is wrapped tightly around her neck. The pearl chains represent the bone ornaments of her iconography.

❀

Solitary Vajrabhairava

Size: 9″
Date: Late 1100s

According to the oral tradition associated with it, this image came to Tibet with Rva Lotsawa, the Tibetan master who translated the Vajrabhairava literature from Sanskrit into Tibetan in the late eleventh century. Rva Lotsawa did much of his work in the Kathmandu Valley, and his cave there is still a pilgrimage place for Tibetans.

The expression on the gold-painted faces and the arrangement of the arms and implements reveals this early Nepalese style. The knife in the right hand resembles the Nepalese dagger called a *khukri*, and is never seen on later Tibetan pieces. The image is an extremely rare and precious piece, and of considerable historical importance.

The Vajrabhairava mandala practice became very popular in Tibet, especially within the Gelukpa school (see page 110).

Vajrabhairava with Consort

Size: 5.5″
Date: Late 1400s

This exquisite miniature sculpture is a form of Vajrabhairava based on the visions of Lama Tsongkhapa. Almost every Gelukpa monk takes its initiation, together with a commitment to perform the daily meditation and mantra recitation for the rest of his or her life.

Here Vajrabhairava is seen with his consort. He is more frequently portrayed in solitary form. The mandala of the "with consort" form is known as "The Thirteen-Deity Vajrabhairava," whereas the Solitary Vajrabhairava mandala has only the one deity. With these exceptions, the structure of the two practices is identical.

Five Miniature Statues

A few years after the creation of Drepung Loseling Monastery in 1416, Chieftain Ganden Tsewang of western Tibet, a disciple of the First Dalai Lama, sponsored the building of a monastery in his kingdom by the name of Ganden Chokhor, which was an affiliate of Drepung Loseling. He also patronized the construction of a large number of artworks for Ganden Chokhor, and encouraged his friends and followers to do the same.

Five miniature images from this period were carried out of Tibet following the destruction of the monastery by the Chinese Communists in 1959. These are excellent examples of the lost wax technique of metal casting employed by Tibetan artists in the period. All these pieces were created between 1420 and 1440.

Buddha in His Sambhogakaya Form

Size: 8.5″

As described in Part One, there are three dimensions to enlightenment: Dharmakaya, Samboghakaya, and Nirmanakaya. The first of these is depicted as a stupa, and also as a simplified buddha image; the third is depicted as a slightly more human and ornate figure; and the Samboghakaya is depicted with the five-pointed crown, ornaments, and so forth.

Sometimes a statue will be made as a Nirmanakaya image, and then later be transformed into a Samboghakaya by offering a crown and ornaments to it. For example, during the Great Prayer Festival of 1410, Lama Tsongkhapa, the founder of the Gelukpa school, did this when he offered a golden crown and ornaments to the holy Jowo statue of the Jokhang, the main temple in Lhasa. This statue had originally been carried to Tibet by King Songtsen Gampo's Chinese wife in the mid-seventh century. It was a Nirmanakaya form, but the crown and ornaments offered by Tsongkhapa transformed it into a Samboghakaya image, and it has remained as such until the present day.

This small Buddha image is a celebration of that adventure.

Guru Padma Sambhava

Size: 5.5"

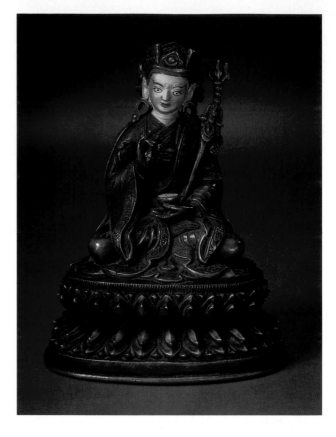

Padma Sambhava, the great guru who came to Tibet in the mid-eighth century and oversaw the construction of Tibet's first monastery, is venerated in all Gelukpa monasteries.

The delicate arrangement of his robe reveals the subtle techniques employed by fifteenth-century artists. Unfortunately, the piece is slightly damaged, and the top of the hat is broken. The gold paint is a recent offering made by a devoted Tibetan.

Avalokiteshvara

Size: 7"

This bronze statue of Avalokiteshvara, the Bodhisattva of Compassion, was commissioned in 1424 by Lama Dampa Sonam Gyaltsen, a fifteenth-century lama of considerable renown from western Tibet. The image has an aura made of bronze mixed with mercury, which was cast separately. The gold paint on the face has been recently offered by a devoted Tibetan.

Vajrasattva

Size: 9″

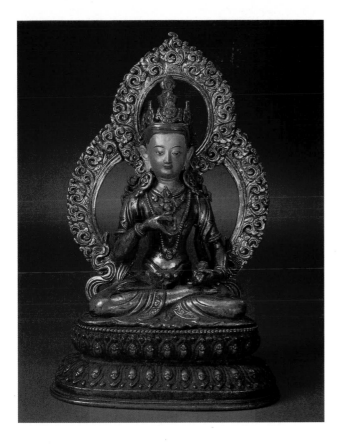

Vajrasattva, the Bodhisattva of Compassion, is a symbol of the power to purify the mind of the instincts of negative karma and delusions, by which the practitioner is released from the guilt of negativities created in the past.

Most Tibetans recite the hundred-syllable Vajrasattva mantra for a few moments every day, together with the meditation/visualization of purifying negativities. More serious practitioners make a two- or three-month retreat sometime in their lives, in which they recite 100,000 of the mantra.

This bronze image was offered to the monastery by Ngawang Drakpa, one of the main soldiers under chieftain Ganden Tzewang.

Manjushri

Size: 7″

Manjushri, the Bodhisattva of Wisdom, is especially popular in the Gelukpa school, for Tsongkhapa was one of his most important Tibetan incarnations.

This image of Manjushri is made of gilded bronze with traces of silver. It was offered by the yogi Naljor Drakpa to the monastery in 1432 in order to increase the wisdom of future generations.

Tsa-tsa Mold of the First Dalai Lama

Size: 6″
Date: Early 1500s

Tsa-tsa, which are small statues made from pressed clay, are found throughout Central Asia. Sometimes a practitioner or devotee will have several thousand made as an act of merit; these would then be placed in a small hut constructed specifically to house them, usually located on a pilgrimage route or on the local *khor-ra* trail (i.e., the "walk-around" circuit that most Tibetans make each morning to circumambulate the local temples, stupas, and monasteries). A few of the tsa-tsas would be painted and used as altar pieces. Sometimes a high lama giving a teaching or initiation has a large number of tsa-tsas made, with one being given to each member of the audience at the conclusion of the event.

Another use for tsa-tsas is as a blessing medium for the dead. The ashes of a cremated person are mixed with clay and pressed into tsa-tsa statues, which then are placed near holy sites.

It is also common for the ashes of a cremated lama to be mixed with clay and made into tsa-tsas. These are then distributed among the lama's disciples and used as personal altar pieces.

The tsa-tsa mold in our exhibit is designed to turn out six-inch clay statues of the First Dalai Lama. This mold apparently was discovered as a hidden treasure, and thus is regarded by Tibetans as having special magical properties.

Three Stupas

A stupa is a symbol of the enlightened mind. Each aspect of its design symbolizes a facet of the enlightenment experience, as well as the path leading to it.

According to Buddhist legend, when the Buddha passed away at the age of eighty, he was cremated and his relics divided between the eight principal groups of his followers. Each of the eight groups enshrined their share of relics in a large reliquary monument, from where they poured out their blessings and acted as objects of devotion and inspiration to future practitioners.

Because there were eight groups who received the relics, the tradition of eight types of stupas arose. These eight developed artistically in India over the centuries, and each came to be identified with a major event in the life of Shakyamuni Buddha. Three of these are exemplified by the three stupas in our exhibit.

The tradition of a stupa as reliquary continued in Tibet. After a deceased lama is cremated, portions of his ashes are placed in two stupas: a large one of earth and stone, which is constructed in a public place and serves as a reminder to the people of the life and deeds of that master; and a smaller one, usually made from metal, that is kept in the temple where the lama resided.

A second usage of the stupa is as an altar piece. Most Tibetan altars have at least three objects on it: a statue or tangka, to represent the body of the Buddha; a text, which represents the speech of the Buddha; and a stupa, to represent the Buddha's mind.

Stupa of Complete Victory

Size: 24"
Date: 1600s

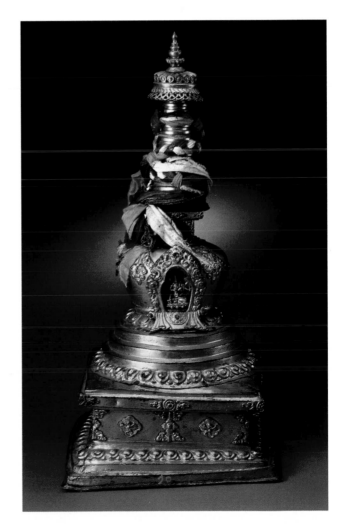

Of the eight types of stupas, this one is in the category known as "The Stupa of Complete Victory," which commemorates the Buddha's extension of his lifespan by means of his meditation. This suggests that it was originally made in order to extend the lifespan of its patron, or as a gift to a lama as a life-extending offering.

Inside the little chapel in the stupa is an image of Ushnisha Vijaya, the goddess of health and longevity.

The four lower steps on the pedestal symbolize the four immeasurable attitudes—love, compassion, sharing in joy, and equanimity—for these are the foundations of the enlightenment path. Above these we see ten steps leading up to the chapel in which the deity sits; these represent the ten stages of development that transport the meditator to enlightenment. The body of the stupa itself represents the dome of enlightenment, which is the awakened mind. The thirteen rings represent the thirteen different styles of conveying the teachings. These are surmounted by a five-petaled lotus, which represents the five wisdoms.

The piece is made of gilded bronze.

Bodhi Stupa

Size: 5″
Date: 1500s

This stupa belongs to the class known as "The Stupa of Many Gates," which commemorates the Buddha's act of teaching and is associated with his first turning of the wheel of Dharma at Sarnath.

A small vajra is tied to the stupa, as it is made from the same material and by the same artist. Possibly it once was an implement held by a tantric deity that was lost centuries ago. The stupa and vajra, however, have remained as companions. They are regarded as objects of great blessing in Loseling, although details of their origins have been lost with the diaspora.

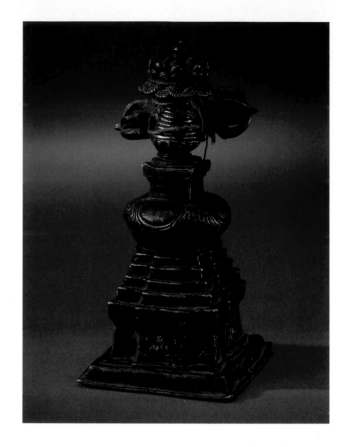

Kadam Stupa

Size: 8.5″
Date: Late 1000s

This bronze stupa is believed to have belonged to one of the main disciples of Atisha Dipamkara Shrijnana, the founder of the Kadam school. It belongs to the class known as "The Stupas of Parinirvana," which commemorates the Buddha's passing away into parinirvana at Kushinagar.

The shape of the stupa indicates that it is a Kadam Stupa, the name given to a special style of stupa introduced into Tibet by Atisha and made popular by the early Kadampa lamas. It is based on the ancient Indonesian tradition, which Atisha encountered during his twelve-year training under the Indonesian Buddhist master Suvarnadvipi Dharmakirti.

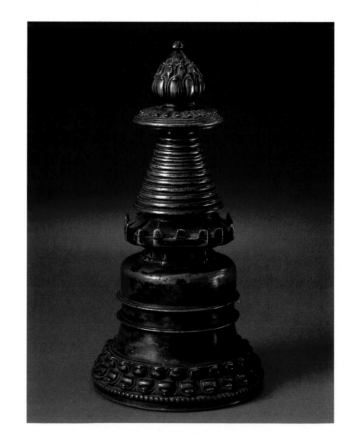

The Names of the Buddha

Size: 5″ x 14″
Date: Late 1300s

This is a copy of the Buddhist sutra popularly referred to by Tibetans as *Sangyey Tsen Boom*, which translates as *The Vase of Names of the Buddha*. The title of the text literally translates as "The 5,853 Names of the Buddha," quite sufficient to fill a vase.

The text has survived the centuries due to the care with which it was prepared six hundred years ago. The paper was first dyed with indigo and orpiment, thus creating the darkness of the surface; after this, arsenic trisulphate was added in order to protect the paper from insects. This was then used as the base on which the scripture was copied.

The text has wooden covers. The top piece is engraved with images of the buddhas of the three times—past, present, and future. Here Buddha Shakyamuni sits in the center and represents the buddhas of the present time. A delicately carved gathering of mythological animals reach out from his aura. Dipamkara, the universal teacher of the previous age, is on his right, to depict the buddhas of the past. Finally, Maitreya sits to his left, and represents the buddhas of the future.

The back cover is decorated with a floral pattern based on the Indo-Tibetan tradition.

The Diamond Sutra

Size: 3.5″ x 11.5″
Date: Mid-1400s

This sutra is in the category of "wisdom discourses" of the Buddha, and presents the doctrine of voidness in wonderful detail.

Our edition is an exquisite example of Tibetan calligraphic work. Here the artist first prepared his paper by dying it with black ink and then adding blue by means of applying an azurite paint. After this the text was copied with lines of ink alternating between gold and silver.

The painted illustrations in the early pages of the text are recent additions.

Eight Ritual Objects

The ritual objects used in tantric meditation have kept Tibetan metal artists busy for centuries. Most of the smaller pieces are made of silver with gold inlay, and are rich in engraved symbols, such as the eight auspicious emblems. The larger pieces are made of bronze or bronze-based alloys.

Mandala Offering Set

Size: 7″ wide; 8″ high when filled
Date: Mid-1800s

The symbolic offering of the universe is performed in conjunction with a "mandala set," which has a base, four sets of rings, and a top ornament. The meditator places the first ring on the base, pours on the appropriate number of handfuls of offering grain, then adds the second ring and more grain, and finally adds the third and fourth ring and more grain. While doing this he or she chants the associated liturgy, which mentions everything from the earth and its treasures up to the sun, moon, and stars. This is then mentally offered to the forces of goodness, with the prayer that all beings be benefited. Most practitioners add semiprecious gems to the grain that is used.

This mandala set is made of silver with inlaid gold, and has the eight auspicious emblems as decorations.

Working Vase

Size: 7.5″ high
Date: Late 1700s

The ritual vase is used in tantric meditation from the time of the initial empowerment, when it plays an important role in the Vase Initiation, up to the stage of a tantric master, when one engages in ritual healings, consecrations, exorcisms, and so forth.

Holy water is sprinkled from the vase throughout the rituals; hence its name, "working vase." This particular vase is made of silver, with abundant gold inlay.

Kapala: The Inner Offering

Size: 7.5″ high
Date: Mid-1800s

"Kapala" means skull, and often the top of a human skull is used for this ritual purpose. The cup of the metal kapala is always made in the shape of a human skull. During tantric meditation the cup is filled with alcohol, which is visualized as having five corpses and five bodily excretions. The meditation transforms these into ambrosia, symbolic of the five delusions of the mind being transformed into the five wisdoms and the five psycho-physical aggregates being transformed into the five buddhas.

This kapala is made of silver with gold inlay.

Torchey: A Spirit Offering Set

Size: Copper bowl, 10.5″ in diameter
Date: Late 1800s

The *torchey* is an elaborate ritual for feeding spirits. It uses a ritual set made of six components. A small silver bowl is placed on a silver stand, which is placed inside a large copper bowl. An offering cake is placed in the silver plate. The ritualist then places the hairpiece over his forehead so that the fringe falls over his eyes, in order to reduce the radiance from his head and eyes, a radiance that frightens away spirits. When the spirits have arrived, he pours water from a copper pot over a spoon held over the vessel; the liquid flows out of the spoon and into the silver vessel. The spirits are satiated and discontinue any spooky activity that they may have been engaged in because of their craving and general irritability.

Water Offering Vase

Size: 12.5″ high
Date: Late 1700s

This ornate vase is made of a copper-based alloy and studded with coral and turquoise. It is used in a number of rituals where consecrated water is required.

Large Ser-kyem Offering Set

Size: Bowl is 18″ wide; goblet is 12″ high;
vase is 24″ high
Date: Mid-1600s

The *ser-kyem* rite is usually done in conjunction with the *sang-chok*, in which juniper branches and sacred substances are burned and the smoke sent to carry prayers and auspicious thoughts on the winds to the four corners of the earth.

During the ser-kyem rite the ritualist pours tea from the vase into the goblet, which stands in the center of the large base vessel. Prayers are sent to the gurus, meditational deities, dakas and dakinis, dharmapalas, and every type of nature spirit, elf, ghost, and goblin. The ritual is undoubtedly of pre-Buddhist origins, although when done in Buddhist monasteries is given a Buddhist perspective. The tea, which in reality is heavenly nectars, flows everywhere, and brings every blessing.

This very old silver set is exquisitely finished, with engravings of the auspicious longevity emblems.

Treasure Dagger

Size: 12.5″ long
Date: 1100s

This ritual dagger is a *ter*, or "treasure," meaning that it was found by a *ter-ton*, or "treasure revealer," a type of Tibetan mystic that specializes in unearthing texts, images, and ritual objects of special power and blessing. In Drepung Loseling it is used for exorcisms and forceful healings whenever an activity of this nature is required.

Five Sets of Musical Instruments

Tibetan tantric music involves the use of numerous instruments. The exhibit includes five types.

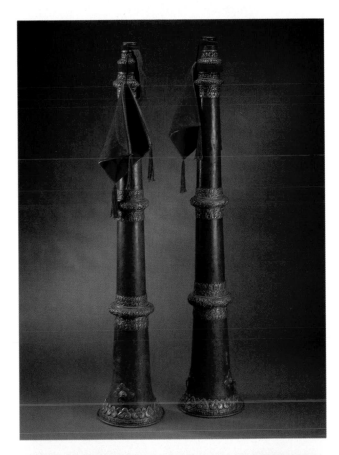

Two Long Horn Trumpets (*dung-chen*)

Size: 115″ long when opened out; 50″ long
when collapsed.
Date: 1800s

The *dung-chen* produces a low, bass note that acts as the undercurrent in Tibetan temple music. Its sound is supposed to resemble the singing of elephants. They are made of copper, with an alloy reinforcer.

Short Horns (*gya-ling*)

Size: 23″ long
Date: 1800s

The *gya-ling* makes a high, piercing sound, and is used as punctuation in temple music. It is a reed instrument, and requires circular breathing. Its sound is supposed to resemble the music of the gods.

Two Metal Thigh Bone Trumpets (*kang-ling*)

Size: 17″ long
Date: 1800s

The *kang-ling* traditionally is a trumpet made of a human thigh-bone. Sometimes a monastery would use a metal lookalike instead, that would produce much the same sound. The bone-shape is intended to remind the player and listener of his own impermanence and death.

Large Cymbals (*boob*)

Size: 13.5″ in diameter
Date: 1800s

The *boob* is a set of two large cymbals used in the propitiation of the dharmapalas. They are made of an alloy of approximately a dozen metals that are specially blended to create a specific sound. They provide both rhythm and melody to temple music, as they make different sounds on different parts of their structure.

Small Cymbals (*ting-sha*)

Size: 3.5″ in diameter
Date: Late 1700s

The set of two small cymbals is made of an alloy composed of twelve different metals. It is used mostly in rituals for appeasing a specific type of ghost.

Utilitarian Objects

A number of utilitarian objects are included in The Mystical Arts of Tibet exhibit, because they exemplify the diversity of Tibetan artists and also because they show how spiritual and mystical values spilled over into all aspects of Tibetan life.

Antique Carpets

Tibet has a long history of carpet-making. Located with Persia to its west, China to its east, and India to its south, it absorbed techniques, styles, and design elements from all three.

The Tibetans used carpets in many ways. The most common was on their beds. Tibetan beds usually doubled as sleepers and sitters. At night the carpet would be rolled up, and the bedding brought out; in the morning the bedding would be put away and the carpet rolled out. Bed carpets are usually approximately three feet wide and six feet long.

Tibet's large nomadic population contributed to the development of the carpet industry and ensured strong support to the weaving artists. Not only did the nomads provide the weavers with a ready supply of high-quality wools, they also acted as an eager market for the woven products. Carpets were wonderfully portable, warm, and beautiful; the nomads used them on the floors of their tents, as horse blankets, and in many other ways.

Temples also patronized the weaving arts. Isle runners up to ten meters long and a meter in width were common. The monks used them on their beds and meditation seats, and they could even be found as door hangings, pillar ornaments, and on teaching thrones.

The pile or tuft used in Tibetan carpets is made mostly of wool from sheep raised in high mountain areas. This wool is preferred because of its coarseness, long fibers, and the silky appearance of the inner hair. It also is much easier to knot.

The Tibetans have a very distinctive style of weaving and knotting. Their production techniques differ from those of the Chinese and Persian traditions, and most likely date to the thirteenth century.

Although carpets are generally thought of as being secular and utilitarian in nature, they are rich in designs of a spiritual symbolism. As in most things Tibetan, the spiritual spills over quietly into the secular world.

Our exhibit includes seven antique carpets from Drepung Loseling, four of which have found space in this catalog.

Dragolion and Phoenofish

Size: 5' 10" long by 3' wide
Date: 1930s

Here the centerpiece is the mythological animal that is a composite of nine auspicious animals. He has the horns of a stag, the forehead of a camel, the eyes of a troll, the neck of a snake, the body of a crocodile, the scales of a carp, the claws of an eagle, the paws of a tiger, and the ears of an ox. He is a symbol of power and the male principle.

To either side of him is a mythological bird having the breast of a wild swan, the back of a unicorn, the throat of a swallow, the bill of a fowl, the neck of a snake, the tail of a fish, the forehead of a crane, the crown of a mandarin, the stripes of a dragon, and the back of a tortoise. These two birds represent the feminine quality. Together with the centerpiece figure the image is of the harmony of male and female.

The border has numerous auspicious symbols, including the endless knot (which contains a variation of the swastika) and lotus flowers.

Dragons and Phoenix Birds

Size: 6' 3" long by 3' 6" wide
Date: Approx. 1910

The image on this carpet depicts two dragons and two phoenix birds playing freely in the sky. The dragons live in the clouds, and make the thunder and lightning that occur during storms; they symbolize the power and intensity of the enlightenment experience. (One rarely meets an elderly Tibetan who does not claim to have seen a dragon at least once in his life.) The phoenix symbolizes victory over negative forces, especially ignorance and anger.

These two couples sport together amidst a rainfall of lotus flowers. All of this occurs within a rainbow border, signifying the beauty and joy of harmonious living.

Three Medallions

Size: 5′ 6″ long by 42′ 9″ wide
Date: 1920s

This carpet contains the image of the three floral medallions, which is a common theme in Tibetan carpets. These represent the natural purity of acts of body, speech, and mind. The blue border design contains a number of traditional elements, including a red flute and a book wrapped in a scarf; these symbolize the value of learning and the arts.

The light beige double-T-shaped border design is known as "the thunder line," and is a variation of the knot of infinity. The dots in the inner row represent a garland of pearls, and signify how beauty is to be found in the most unlikely of places by the one who knows how to look correctly.

Cryanthynum and Auspicious Emblems

Size: 5′ 10″ x 3′ x 2″ wide
Dates: 1890s

The cryanthynum in Buddhism is a symbol of gentleness, beauty and prosperity. Four butterflies (a Tibetan pre-Picasso stylization) play in the four corners. The butterfly represents transformation, rebirth, and beauty emerging from ugliness. Two knots of infinity (a variation of the swastika) and two seals stand in the subdivisions.

Katas, or auspicious offering scarves, flow in the borders and inner frame. Other auspicious emblems, like trinkets of the gods, also adorn the border.

Brazier and Teapot

Size: Brazier is 12″ high; pot is 13″ high
Date: Mid-1800s

Tibetans were great tea-drinkers. As many travelers to Tibet have remarked, it is impossible to visit a Tibetan household and leave without drinking several cups of "yak butter tea," with the butter invariably being somewhat rancid. Tibetans always get a giggle out of this expression, because the yak is male; its female counterpart is called the *dri*.

The beverage is made by bringing the water to a boil, allowing it to cook for a few moments, and then adding butter, salt, a pinch of soda, and a hint of milk. The mixture is beaten in a churn, and then kept in a pot on the stove and consumed as desired.

Alternatively, it could be kept on a brazier, such as this. Hot charcoals are put in the lower container, and the teapot is placed on top. In addition to keeping the tea hot, it brings an added warmth to the room.

Set of Tibetan Currency

The currency of Tibet was colorful and reflected the unique Tibetan structure of combining spiritual and temporal elements in their leadership. The paper currency bears the name of the Lhasa government: "The Joyous Tushita Mansion Uniting Spiritual and Temporal Concerns." Tushita is the name of Maitreya Buddha's pure land.

Both coins and paper money came in a variety of denominations, and had numerous auspicious and mystical symbols on them. This paper currency depicts two snow lions holding up a tray of offerings; these two symbolize keeping both the body and the mind strong and balanced.

Antique Saddle

Size: 23″ long by 12″ high at the horn
Date: Mid-1600s

This extraordinary saddle, with silver horn, silver-alloy stirrups, and gilded headpiece, is believed to have belonged to the Fifth Dalai Lama and been used by him between 1640 and 1650. It shows exquisite workmanship in the metalwork.

Traditional Jewelry

Tibetan jewelry is made largely with silver and gold, with a great variety of precious and semi-precious stones. Coral and turquoise are their favorite stones, but many others are used. Tibetans believe that wearing these substances attracts the spirits of prosperity, and balances the body's aura.

The exhibit contains three such pieces: (1) a gold pendant studded with turquoise and worn on a string of semi-precious stones; (2) a silver necklace with turquoise and coral beads; and (3) a plain silver necklace. The pennant would be used as a case for blessing substances, holy relics, and lama medicines.

SECTION THREE:
THE TRADITION CONTINUES

Silk Applique Tangka
of the Buddha

Size: 4' 10" by 7' 9"

This is a wonderful example of one of the artforms most admired by Tibetans. The silk applique technique is held in high regard throughout Central Asia, and was used in the production of the enormous images used at festivals. Some tangkas were a hundred feet and more in length, and on special occasions were hung from the rooftops of monasteries.

The central figure in this work is the Buddha. Two of the greatest Indian masters sit below him: Nagarjuna to his right (the viewer's left); and Asanga to his left. Tibetans call these two masters *Chok-nyi,* or "The Two Supreme Ones," and regard them as the two most important Buddhist masters from early India. They are surpassed in the veneration that they receive only by the Buddha himself. Nagarjuna was the principal Indian elucidator of Buddha's teachings on voidness, and Asanga was the principal elucidator of Buddha's teachings on the general bodhisattva trainings that constitute the Universal Vehicle.

We have seen both Nagarjuna and Asanga mentioned in the first two tangkas of Section Two, the Lam Rim Assembly Tree and Lama Chopa Assembly Tree, where Nagarjuna acts as the principal Indian recipient of the "Lineage of the Profound View," or Buddha's teachings on emptiness, and Asanga acts as the principal recipient of the "Lineage of the Extensive Bodhisattva Activities," or Buddha's general teachings on the bodhisattva trainings.

Nagarjuna's life and deeds is said to have been prophesied by the Buddha himself in the *Lankavatara Sutra,* wherein he said, "Four hundred and fifty years after my passing a man will come from South India from the land where the beda grass grows. His name will be Juna, and he will vastly propagate my inner teachings."

Nagarjuna is always depicted with naga snakes rising from behind his shoulders, because he made a six year retreat in a cave in the Kathmandu Valley, where he met with the nagas and received the *Prajna Paramita Sutras,* the essence of Buddha's teachings on emptiness. The nagas lived in a lake in the inner confines of the cave.

In ordinary parlance nagas are serpent spirits. In Buddhist mystical language the term refers to aryas, or saints. Nagarjuna received the emptiness teachings from them, and then propagated these widely throughout India. In the Lam Rim tradition it is said that he received the wisdom teachings directly from Manjushri, because during this retreat he experienced constant visions in which Manjushri appeared to him and clarified the meaning of the *Prajna Paramita Sutras.*

He also composed many treatises on the emptiness doctrine, which achieved widespread popularity. The impact of his work was so pervasive that often he is referred to as the Father of the Mahayana. All Mahayana schools of Buddhism descend from him, although philosophically he is regarded as the forefather of the Madhyamaka schools. In Drepung Loseling Monastery his *Prajnamula,* together with its commentaries, is studied for three years.

Asanga, who was also from South India and appeared two centuries after Nagarjuna's birth, became famous because of four three-year retreats that he made. After each of the first three of these he became disheartened at his progress, but renewed his efforts, and eventually achieved realization. The many texts that he wrote, especially those based on his visions of Maitreya, achieved instant popularity. As a writer he took the many *Prajna Paramita Sutras,* extracted their essence, and presented all the ideas and practices taught in them in forms suited to systematic study. The *Abhisamaya-alamkara,* one of the five texts that he received in his visions of Maitreya, is studied in Drepung Loseling for a period of seven years.

The two together are regarded as the earlier Indian formulators of the Mahayana movement, that was to sweep North India, and from there spread throughout China, Korea, Japan and Vietnam, and later take root in Tibet and Mongolia.

Ganden Lha Gyama

Size: 25.5" x 37"
Date: Early 1900s

The Tibetan name for this tangka, *Ganden Lha Gyama*, or "The Hundred Divinities of Tushita Pure Land," is derived from the first line of the liturgy used in the conjunction with the meditation represented by the image. The liturgy reads, "From the heart of the lord of the hundreds of divinities of Tushita Pure Land/ On a carpet of milky white billowing clouds/ Come forth, O great Dharma Lord Omniscient Tsongkhapa/ Together with your chief disciples."

Here "the lord of the hundreds of divinities of Tushita Pure Land" refers to Maitreya Buddha, who is depicted sitting on a throne in the top center of the painting. The two figures in front of him to his right and left are Atisha and Tsongkhapa, respectively, the founders of the Kadampa and Gelukpa schools. The three central figures are Tsongkhapa and his two chief disciples, the elderly Gyaltsab Jey and the younger Khedrub Jey.

In the daily meditation, these three figures are visualized as emanating from Maitreya's heart and coming forth on a blanket of clouds. They take their place in the space in front of the meditator. He or she then chants the seven verses known as "the seven-limbed worship" (i.e., one verse each for prostrations, making offerings, purification of negative karma, rejoicing in the goodness of oneself and others, asking the masters to remain in the world, asking them to teach, and dedication of merit), and engages in the mantra recitation and meditation. When done as a retreat, the practice takes approximately a month to complete.

In front of the central figures is a table with the standard seven offerings: the two waters for purification and the five sense objects. In the sky above we see various gods and goddesses making offerings, with the former being to Tsongkhapa's right and the latter to his left. Three dharmapalas stand at the bottom of the composition and offer their services of protection: Kalarupa (right), Mahakala (center), and Vaishravana (left). We have seen them in several tangkas described in Section One, and the reader can refer to them there.

The twenty-fifth day of the tenth month of every Tibetan year is known to Tibetans as *Ganden Namchu*, or "The Ganden Twenty-fifth." Western writers usually refer to it as "The Butterlamp Festival," for on this day Tibetans annually burn millions of butterlamps. The rooftops of temples and households, as well as the precincts of monasteries, temples, and sacred "walkaround" sites, are all made resplendent with rows of dozens, hundreds, or even thousands of butterlamps. The focus of the festival is the Ganden Lhagyama practice depicted in this tangka. During the day everyone chants the mantra of the practice and meditates. At night they run around fervently keeping the butterlamps filled, holding bundles of insence in their hands and singing the mantra melodically.

The mantra itself is recited in Tibetan; this is unlike most mantras, which are done in Sanskrit. In fact it is a verse composed of five nine-syllable lines, with the theme being how Tsongkhapa was an embodiment of the three principal bodhisattvas—Avalokiteshvara, Manjushri and Vajrapani—and of the three qualities that these bodhisattvas symbolize: compassion, wisdom and power. There is a three-volume Tibetan collection of books on the various meditations that can be done in conjunction with the mantra. Perhaps the most common is as follows. As the first line is chanted one meditates that the syllable *om* comes from Tsongkhapa's forehead to one's own, bringing with it the blessings of Avalokiteshvara and reinforcing one's compassion. As the second line is chanted the syllable *ah* comes from Tsongkhapa's throat to one's own, bringing the blessings of Manjushri and reinforcing one's wisdom. As the third line is said a blue *hum* comes from Tsongkhapa's heart to one's own, bringing the blessings of Vajrapani and increasing one's personal power. The final two lines of the verse cause these three qualities to become fully absorbed into one's mindstream, and one becomes an embodiment of compassion, wisdom and power.

The Butterlamp Festival is an especially joyous event for children, who sing the mantra loudly, melodically and playfully as they race about relighting any butterlamps that have become blown out by the wind.

Buddha Shakyamuni

Size: 19″

Guru Padma Sambhava

19″

Manjushri, the Bodhisattva of Wisdom

Size: 18.5″

Avalokiteshvara, the Bodhisattva of Compassion

Size: 19″

Tara, the Bodhisattva of Enlightenment Activity

Size: 18.5″

Vajrasattva, the Bodhisattva of Purification

Size: 17″

Vajrayogini

Size: 14″

The Three Bodhisattvas

Size: 19″
One thousand armed Avalokiteshvara in center, with Manjushri to his right and Vajrapani to his left. Made of silver.

Set of Two Ceremonial Tea Cups
Size: 8.25″ high
Silver

Triku Ritual Knife
Size: 6.8″
Bronze alloy

Vajra and Bell Set
Size: Vajra is 5″; bell is 7.5″
Li alloy and bronze

Kapala
Size: 6.8″ high
Silver

Grain Offering Bowl
Size: 6.8″ high
Silver

Ritual Vase
Size: 7.25″ high
Silver

Mystic Dagger
Size: 7.75″ long
Li alloy

Butterlamp
Size: 8″ high
Silver

Waterbowl Set, with Butterlamp and Mandala Offering Set
Size: 5.5″ diameter, 8″ high, and 8″ diameter, respectively
Silver

Contemporary Carpets

After going into exile, the Tibetans continued to make their carpets. Factories dedicated to this art can be found in every Tibetan refugee settlement in India and Nepal. Carpet-making became so successful in Nepal that by the mid-1970s Nepalese and Indian businessmen began to set up their own factories and imitate the process.

Two new carpets made by refugees are included in our exhibit, to demonstrate the continuation of the weaving arts.

Tiger Rug

Size: 6′ x 9′

The tiger rug was a favorite design with lamas and meditators. Many of the tantric yogis and yoginis of ancient India had used tiger skins as their meditation seats; the Tibetans liked the idea, but preferred to use wool woven to resemble the skin.

This carpet has a tiger skin design in the center, with a light beige checked design as a border. The top and bottom have stylized clouds and a radiant rainbow.

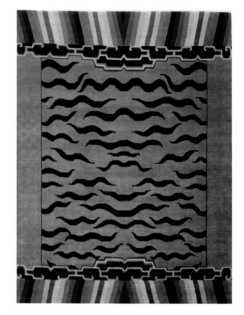

Two Phoenix Birds, Two Dragons, and a Lotus

Size: 6′ x 10′

This rug has a checkered design in its border, and two phoenix birds and two dragons play around a lotus in the center.

The dragon represents male energy, and the phoenix female energy. The lotus represents the place at which the two meet. In tantric symbolism this would be the chakra, at the center of the heart.

Bibliography

(1) Tibetan Cultural and Social History

Batchelor, Stephen, *The Tibet Guide*, Wisdom Publications, 1987

Bell, Sir Charles, *Tibet: Past and Present*, Oxford University Press, 1924

————*The People of Tibet*, Oxford University Press, 1928

Coleman, Graham, *A Handbook of Tibetan Culture*, Rupa & Co., 1993

Mullin, Glenn H., *Life and Teachings of the Thirteenth Dalai Lama*, Snow Lion Publications, 1988

————*Mystical Verses of a Mad Dalai Lama*, Quest Books, 1994

Richardson, Hugh E., *Tibet and Its History*, Shambhala, 1984

Shakabpa, W. D., *Tibet: A Political History*, Yale University Press, 1967

Snellgrove and Richardson, *A Cultural History of Tibet*, Frederick A. Praeger Publishers, 1968

Stein, R.A., *Tibetan Civilization*, Stanford University Press, 1972

(2) Tibetan Art

Clark, Walter E. *Two Lamaist Pantheons*, Harvard University Press, 1965

Lauf, Detlef Ingo, *Tibetan Sacred Art: The Heritage of Tantra*, Shambhala 1976

Olschak, Blanche, and Geshe Thupten Wangyal, *Mystic Art of Ancient Tibet*, McGraw-Hill Publishing Co., 1973

Olson, Eleanor, *Catalogue of the Tibetan Collection and Other Lamaist Articles in the Newark Museum*, 5 Vols., Newark Museum, 1950-71

Pal, Pratapaditya, *Tibetan Paintings*, Ravi Kumar/Sotheby Publications, 1984
————*The Art of Tibet: A Catalogue of the Los Angeles County Museum of Art Collection*, L.A. County Museum of Art, 1983
————*The Art of Tibet: Exhibition Catalogue*, Asia House, New York, 1969
————*Indo-Asian Art from the John Gilmore Ford Collection*, exhibition catalog, The Walters Art Gallery, 1971

Raghuvira and Lokeshchandra, *A New Tibeto-Mongol Pantheon*, 20 Vols., Indian Academy for Indian Culture, 1961-72

Rhie, Marylin M., and Thurman, Robert A., *Wisdom and Compassion: The Sacred Art of Tibet*, Harry N Abrams, 1991

Roreich, George, *Tibetan Paintings*, Paul Guethner, 1925

Tucci, Guiseppe., *The Theory and Practice of the Mandala*, Rider, 1961

————*Tibetan Painted Scrolls*, La Libreria Dello Stato, 1949

Tulku, Tarthang, *The Sacred Art of Tibet*, Dharma Press, 1972

❀❀❀

All quotations from H.H. the Dalai Lama are from private interviews with the author, Glenn H. Mullin.

Photography Credits:

All photographs Part One, Courtesy of

The Tibet Image Bank,
5 Torrens Street,
London EC1Z INQ
England

Photographers:—

Robin Bath — pages 27, 39, 53

Russell Johnson — page 3

Norma Joseph — page 2

Mani Lama — pages 4, 10, 14

David Lewiston — page 58

John Miles — pages 12, 15, 17, 40, 46, 69

Dr. Lloyd Nick — Cover, 9

Irene Siegt — page 7

Nick Veedros — page 72

John Werner — page 67

Bard Wrisley — page 32, 61, 63, 66

All photographs Part Two, Courtesy of Bard Wrisley.

THE MYSTICAL ARTS OF TIBET EXHIBITION
Management Office
Suite 56473
2625 Piedmont Road
Atlanta, Georgia 30324
TEL. / FAX: 404-816-5635
E-mail: www.drepung.org